New Perspectives on Happiness and Mental Wellbeing in Schoolchildren

New Perspectives on Happiness and Mental Wellbeing in Schoolchildren presents a revolutionary approach to handling social rejection during the latency period. It offers the reader an innovative educational approach, adapted to this pre-adolescent age group, for systemic intervention in classes experiencing negative social phenomena. Presenting latency as a significant developmental stage, it explains children's cruelty in social rejection from a developmental perspective.

The book presents the "Envelopes" therapy method to improve children's status immediately and proposes a school intervention for social rejection. It also offers an educational approach appropriate to the developmental needs of latency age children. The approaches described are based on a new developmental psychology paradigm that can illuminate latency with far-reaching insights that aid in adapting approaches suitable to this age. This new paradigm of significant and unique intrapsychic development during early childhood asserts that the most important human development occurs during latency.

With informative case studies used throughout, this book will be of great interest to academics and researchers in the fields of clinical psychology, educational psychology, and teacher training.

Hannah Fisher-Grafy is an expert educational psychologist, psychotherapist, bibliotherapist, and doctoral student studying children's morality.

New Perspectives on Happiness and Mental Wellbeing in Schoolchildren

A Developmental-Psychoanalytical Explanation of the Latency Stage

Hannah Fisher-Grafy

Translated by Ruth Ludlam

Routledge
Taylor & Francis Group

LONDON AND NEW YORK

First published in English 2019
by Routledge
2 Park Square, Milton Park, Abingdon, Oxon OX14 4RN

and by Routledge
605 Third Avenue, New York, NY 10017

First issued in paperback 2020

Routledge is an imprint of the Taylor & Francis Group, an informa business

Translated by Ruth Ludlam

British Library Cataloguing-in-Publication Data
A catalogue record for this book is available from the British Library

Library of Congress Cataloging-in-Publication Data
Names: Fisher-Grafy, Hannah, author.
Title: New perspectives on happiness and mental wellbeing in
    schoolchildren : a developmental-psychoanalytical explanation
    of the latency stage / Hannah Fisher-Grafy.
Description: Abingdon, Oxon ; New York, NY : Routledge, 2019. |
    Includes bibliographical references.
Identifiers: LCCN 2019002115 (print) | LCCN 2019011460 (ebook) |
    ISBN 9780429434181 (eBook) | ISBN 9781138358751 (hbk) |
    ISBN 9780429434181 (ebk)
Subjects: LCSH: School children—Mental health—Case studies. |
    Happiness in children—Case studies. | School children—
    Psychology—Case studies. | Child development—Psychology—
    Case studies.
Classification: LCC LB3430 (ebook) | LCC LB3430 .F57 2019 (print) |
    DDC 371.7/13—dc23
LC record available at https://lccn.loc.gov/2019002115

ISBN 13: 978-0-367-73069-7 (pbk)
ISBN 13: 978-1-138-35875-1 (hbk)

Typeset in Times New Roman
by Apex CoVantage, LLC

To my father, Shlomo Shenkar, who was left one day, at the age of 6, completely alone in a dark world, and who gave all he had to his children.

And to my mother, Dr. Fisher-Abkovitz, of blessed memory, whose image appears in my window to provide guidance.

Contents

Acknowledgments

I would like to thank Ruth Ludlam for her wonderful translation, her dedicated, sensitive, and faithful approach to the manuscript she translated.

Thanks to Dr. Ety Berant, who constitutes an ideal, beloved image for me.

Thanks to my children, Yasmin, Ayelet-Chen, and Eilon; to my sons-in-law, Shani and Yiftach; and to my grandchildren, Lia, Emmanuel, Ya'ara, Zohar, and Ido, for whom my world glows.

And finally, thanks to my beloved husband, Arnon, who believes in the great privilege I have received from the Almighty to bring a new message to the world.

Preface

Social rejection, for all its cruelty, is an essential organ in the emotional development of latency age children. It is part of a complex system without which the entire psychic system during latency wouldn't move and develop. This developmental understanding differs from and opposes the currently existing approach and breaks new ground in both individual therapy for children suffering from social rejection and systematic school treatment of cases of social rejection.

In this book, I present a developmental paradigm that emerged during my experience treating children who suffered from social rejection, both in the context of the Educational Psychological Service, where I managed intervention and social therapy projects in elementary school classes, and in my private clinic. My path as a therapist led to the formation of a new approach regarding both latency and the phenomenon of social rejection. According to this approach, social rejection is normative when it is brief and temporary. In the normative, common social rejection, the rejected children rapidly return to proper social functioning once they recover, adapt, and continue their latency stage development. In contrast, severe social rejection, when it is cruel toward the rejected child and becomes long-term or chronic, indicates an impairment at the earlier emotional development stages, leading to difficulty in the transition to the latency stage.

According to the understanding presented in this book, a change of approach is required for all those involved in treatment and intervention for social rejection: the education system as a whole, principals, homeroom teachers, counselors, therapists, and parents. This new understanding is so innovative and different from the existing approaches that when I first teach it and explain it to educational psychologists, therapists, educational counselors, educators, and the parents of children who come for therapy, some of them find it difficult to accept at first and show resistance. This new paradigm undermines the foundations that have been fixated during the past century regarding educating and treating latency stage children and lays new foundations for understanding this age group. I can note, happily, that when they witness how greatly this understanding enables a change and improvement in the children's situation, they accept it with love, amazement, and gratitude. The new understanding presented in the book is different and sometimes opposed to the current treatment of latency issues such as: conformity, social pressure, leadership, excellence, individualism, negative class norms, behavioral issues, parental intervention, teacher intervention, social skills, social rejection, class rulers, and so on.

This approach shines new light into a new, hidden, and unknown space. It pierces the darkness of a century of psychoanalysis, during which time the latency stage was indeed latent.

Sigmund Freud, the father of psychology, in his shocking and thrilling discoveries regarding the stages of psychological development, famously classified latency (defined as ages 6–12) as a "period" rather than a "stage". Rona Knight (2014) reviewed a century of psychoanalytic treatment of latency and indicated that Freud, who guided the way latency was perceived, saw latency as a period separating the early development stages from the adolescence stage, whose main purpose was developing defense mechanisms as a continuing solution to the Oedipal crisis. Freud viewed the latency age, when there is a decline in sexual activity, as a desexualization of object relations and emotions (Laplanche & Pontalis, 1988). Most of Freud's heirs saw latency as a continuation of the psychosexual development described by Freud. Miriam Williams (1972) saw latency as a continuation of the early development, a sort of lengthening of the previous stage and strengthening of the superego. Other theorists expanded upon the importance of the defense mechanisms as the central characteristic of latency (Becker, 1974; Sarnoff, 1976). According to the Object Relations Theory (Fairbairn, 1946; Klein, 1958) and the Separation Individuation Theory (Mahler, Pine, & Bergman, 1975), during latency there is continued development of children's autonomy and separateness that enables them to separate from home and handle the surroundings outside home, namely the school environment, more independently. Winnicott (1962), as part of his perception of the developmental process, also saw latency as a transition from absolute dependence to relative dependence. Thus, it appears that the psychoanalytical theories from Freud onward treat latency using the same terms and explanations with which they describe the earlier stages in their developmental theories. None of the psychoanalytical approaches treat latency as a developmental stage in which new and significant development occurs that differs essentially and uniquely from the development during earlier stages.

Freud, and later psychoanalysis, not only viewed latency as a period in which no significant development occurred that was unique to this stage, but also considered the achievements of earlier stages to be doomed to regression during latency (Freud, 1926: 210). Indeed, in many areas, during latency a regression in development has been found, forming a U-curve (Nucci & Turiel, 2009). But according to the understanding presented in this book, one of human beings' most impressive developments occurs during latency. True, the psychological dynamic involving corporeality, the erogenous organs, sexuality, drives, the libido, and the id at the earlier stages disappears during latency and reawakens during adolescence. However, a new psychological part of the self emerges that is unrelated to corporeality and drives and has essentially different psychological energies that do not stem from bodily sexual sources. This part is social and is the foundation of the spiritual element in human beings. So, while it is valid to argue that the psychological development that combines physicality, drives, sensuality, sexuality, and emotionality does indeed cease and even regress during latency, it is replaced by a new psychological spirit based on a social self whose existence is in a community, which during latency is the society of classmates. The community, society's foundation, is the environmental basis for the psychic development of the ascension of the human spirit, starting during adolescence, in which individuals move out of the drives of the ego and soar to the expanses of a human spirit of solidarity, fraternity, and love of others, to the unique human spiritual spaces where humankind's sublime spiritual flourishing occurs.

According to the psychological understanding presented in this book, between the ages of 6 and 12, children undergo a developmental stage, latency, in which they have unique needs that require adults – parents, teachers, and therapists – to understand them. This is an axiom in the various deficiency theories: people whose needs are satisfied are calm and happy and continue to develop optimally, while those whose needs are not satisfied are restless, hungry, and irritable, and their development is deficient and delayed. Therefore, this book presents the developmental process that children undergo during latency and their developmental needs at this stage, and, accordingly, introduces an individual therapy ("Envelopes Therapy"), a school intervention for social rejection, and a suitable overall educational approach.

The developmental paradigm of the latency age was formulated during a journey full of hardships in treating socially rejected latency age children. According to this paradigm, three psychic essences exist in the human soul, and during latency only one of them is active. One essence, which is blocked during latency, is the childhood self. This essence is psychological-bodily, drive-based, rigid and inflexible, finite, and deterministic. In it, the self operates using the psychic values of the early developmental stages (up to the end of the Oedipal stage). The second essence, which is active during latency, is the social self. It is flexible and non-committal, essentially spiritual, mental, and infinite. Between these two essences operates an intermediate layer that functions like a membrane between two parts of a cell. During latency, the membrane blocks the self core, where the childhood self essence exists, and makes it unavailable to our consciousness. In latency, the membrane doesn't function at its full capacity, but from adolescence and throughout the rest of our lives, the membrane transfers, mediates, and translates between the two parts of the self, the childhood self and the social self.

Treating latency age children taught me that during latency the childhood self is blocked. The drive-based, sexual, finite, and deterministic part is blocked, while the self moves to exist in the new part, the social self, which is intellectual, social, subject to a system of cold considerations of power struggles and social interests, and has completely different psychic behavioral rules than the childhood self. I discovered the extreme view whereby there is no contact at all between the two parts of the self – meaning that existing in one part doesn't allow simultaneous existence in the other part of the self – from the words of my patients, who repeatedly demonstrated that it's impossible to exist within the reality of the social self when early contents of the childhood self remain conscious. This understanding will be presented and demonstrated in an example later in the book.

According to the paradigm presented in this book, I will offer an educational approach that is shockingly innovative, where the entire burden of education is delegated to the society of children. The significant adults gradually vacate the central stage in favor of the society of children, which becomes the environment for the children's life and the basis for their development at this age. The society of children during latency is the object/selfobject/significant entity. The adults who are significant to infants (parents, kindergarten teachers, teachers) are gradually pushed into the margins of psychic existence and continue to constitute a source of nurturing and support for the early stages of development. Additionally, during latency they serve as a quiet and secure presence that grants power and confidence for the independent existence of the society of children in which the souls of the latency age children develop.

According to the paradigm presented in this book, in individual therapy and in school intervention, social rejection isn't considered as a phenomenon indicating a pathology of the rejected child or of the "cruel" or "bad" classmates, but as healthy, normative development that is essential for the developmental process and should be treated accordingly, thus reducing the severity of the harm. The society of children at this age determines arbitrary social norms that differ from adult morality and that make no reference to the morality of society as a whole. The society of children at this age doesn't respond with empathy to the suffering of rejected children but acts in cold blood in various situations. However, these are certainly not "cruel" children, but children undergoing a developmental stage that expands the human soul to a spiritual dimension, one based on a social system. The latency stage shows us that people, unlike animals, exist on the basis of a system of agreed, uniform social rules that are changeable and often lack justification and existential logic. These are rules that don't take personal factors into account, rules that society itself determines and enforces. Social existence requires its members to behave uniformly, in "group twinship".

Latency teaches us that the moral facet, which is added to development at this stage, is different from the divine orders granted by an external supreme authority. Children during latency obey social norms that are essentially different from divine laws, but which demand no less obedience. Social norms add the most essential dimension of the human spirit: infinite freedom of choice. The human spirit is not merely animal sensation and instinct, which obeys or disobeys a supreme command, good nature versus evil nature. Latency adds to this deterministic choice an infinity of options for moral decisions depending on an infinity of environmental, social, and cultural factors. The latency age adds to our human morality a dimension that, when it is self-standing, as in latency, and is not connected to the earlier and later stages' morality, is a dimension of cold, intellectual choice influenced by social factors, interests, and power struggles. These lead children at this age to make "cruel" moral decisions that are difficult to digest. However, this link in the chain of moral development stages grants to human beings the possibility of moral freedom of choice, which is on the one hand intuitive, emotional, and conscience-driven, and on the other hand subject to utilitarian judgment, a system of social considerations, and cold, intellectual justification. This approach will be clearly expanded upon in this book.

References

Becker, T.E. (1974). On latency. *Psychoanalytic Study of the Child*, 29: 3–11.

Fairbairn, W.R.D. (1946). Object-relationships and dynamic structure. *International Journal of Psychoanalysis*, 27: 30–37.

Freud, S. (1926). The question of lay analysis: Conversations with an impartial person. *Standard Edition*, 20: 183–258.

Klein, M. (1958). On the development of mental functioning. *International Journal of Psychoanalysis*, 39: 84–90.

Knight, R. (2014). A hundred years of latency: From Freudian psychosexual theory to dynamic systems nonlinear development in middle childhood. *Journal of the American Psychoanalytic Association*, 62(2): 203–235.

Laplanche, J. & Pontalis, J. (1988). *The Language of Psychoanalysis*. London: Karnac Books.

Mahler, M.S., Pine, F., & Bergman, A. (1975). *The Psychological Birth of the Human Infant: Symbiosis and Individuation*. New York: Basic Books.

Nucci, L. & Turiel, E. (2009). Capturing the complexity of moral development and education. *Mind, Brain, and Education*, 3(3): 151–159.

Sarnoff, C. (1976). *Latency*. New York: Aronson.

Williams, M. (1972). Problems of technique during latency. *Psychoanalytic Study of the Child*, 27: 598–617.

Winnicott, D.W. (1962). The theory of the parent-infant relationship: Contributions to discussion. *International Journal of Psychoanalysis*, 43: 256–257.

Introduction

Perhaps this sounds like a fantasy or fictional scenario. Children wake up in the morning and want to go to school, which is a place of joyful growth for them. They pass through the school gates feeling wonderful. An entrance full of expectations. They calmly place their bags beside their desks and go out during recess feeling confident and excited, play happily during the break, and return to class with the same excitement.

Is it possible that our whole perception of the world of schoolchildren is flawed? If so, isn't it time we reached this conclusion? Children suffering at school are not rare. In fact, too many children dislike going to school. Unfortunately, many children even suffer from their time there. They suffer as a result of their classes, their friends, their teachers. Many teachers, just like the children, are also unhappy when they go to school. Teachers expend significant efforts in making the children feel good at school. But, like the children, despite their efforts to cope with all the daily tasks they face in school, they come home feeling empty, that something wasn't going well, or that the children were too wild, or that they shouted and punished too much, or that they were bullied by one of the children, or the parents, or the principal. . . . So, why, in our modern and developed world, with so much information and so many possibilities, do so many children and teachers suffer at school? Why is this the end result, after all the effort invested by the school's faculty?

Happy schoolchildren are not children for whom a rare, private, expensive setting has been found. Not children the school entertains with interesting subjects, not those lucky enough to have a good homeroom teacher, not those given roles and empowered, or those whose school has an impressive educational agenda. Their happiness doesn't result from external factors. They're happy because that's their basic, internal state. They're happy because school is a growing environment suited to their developmental needs. Happy schoolchildren don't require large budgets or great efforts. Only one thing is required: to understand what schoolchildren need and to provide for these needs.

So, what do schoolchildren need?

They need fulfillment of the significant need of their current developmental stage – the latency stage – which is social nourishment. In other words, nourishment from the autonomous society of classmates.

The society of children during latency becomes autonomous: a body of children with a hierarchy, its own rules, and a system of enforcement and punishment. This is a cohesive society, structured and organized, which responds as one, autonomously, and which is not guided by external factors such as parents and teachers. Its behavior and motion stem from within it and are uniform and independent. During latency, this autonomous society of children nourishes the children's developmental needs; the selfobject needs of grandiosity, idealization, and twinship; and also the need of developing the psychic function of subordination.

Any activity, encounter, or learning originates from the understanding that children have a need for social nourishment, that this is the most significant need at elementary school age, and that it is very powerful. This is in contrast with the early stages of development when parents and family were the selfobject and the main providers of the young infants' needs. Elementary school, from second grade to fifth grade, is the main framework where children receive nourishment for their developmental needs. Therefore, the school's most important role is to fulfill this essential need for children of this age group. Satisfying this need will lead children to feel that their environment is nourishing them with calm and unexceptional adaptiveness that enables their proper development. I wish to make a surprising claim, that all children – even the anomalous ones, whom the education system often has difficulty in containing, and who are frequently transferred from normal settings to special education settings, children with learning difficulties, delays, and deficits – can feel the same happiness at school, in the society of ordinary children, when it is based on a developmental understanding of this age.

How can we do this? How can we fulfill the central developmental need of latency?

First, we have to position the school as an environment that enables nourishing of the children's developmental-social need, and not as happens at present, with the school fulfilling the adults' need for academic achievements, educating for discipline and obedience, and social activities with educational value – as the adults perceive it. Second, everything that happens at school should be founded upon the children's need to conduct a social life, as a group, independently. The society of children becomes the significant selfobject for children at this age, determining the norms, the order, the nature of the breaks and the lessons. This might sound fictional, because we are used to seeing adults as the selfobjects solely responsible for educating and teaching children. This approach seems likely to raise objections. Is it possible to do this? But fifth-grade children are not only capable of doing this, they are thirsty to do this, they need this, and in fact, they must do this, for the sake of developing their good separateness.

The intention is not to create a society of children isolated on an island of children with no adults, of chaos and disorder. Social nourishment doesn't remove the adults from school life, but the nature of the adult presence must change. It must be directed to create and form a developmental environment that enables the society of classmates to act as an independent group, according to its internal social order, with a hierarchy and rules that are purely its own creation.

Such a social order must also include the difficult phenomenon of social rejection. Social rejection fulfills the need for the existence of an enforcement tool of the society of children to create social uniformity, which is so essential for social belonging. However, social rejection should be handled delicately, since it is not an evil or a disease that should be fought, treated, and healed, whether the rejected child or the society of children who reject him or her. Social rejection is actually a very powerful tool – the only one with influence and power at this age – and it constitutes the whip through which the society of children disciplines those who are not meeting the developmental pace, and helps them get onto the developmental track, to continue to the next stop of adolescence.

As a normative phenomenon belonging to the developmental stage, every child in elementary school has experienced normative social rejection (Binstock, 2003). All children at this age experience a situation where a group of children doesn't share with them, attacks them, hurts them, treats them unfairly and unjustly, misunderstands them, treats them with contempt, isolates them, or marginalizes them out of social activity. The difference is in the frequency and the severity, but all children are familiar with the experience. The phenomenon is so common that there is no school that isn't engaged in finding solutions to these difficult social situations, but still, professionals feel helpless in handling it. Again and again we hear about shocking cases of abuse among children. Whenever such a case arises, the public is outraged, vilifying the cruel children, calling them "monsters", "heartless", "a bad class", "a cruel class". The education system comes under attack and acts under great pressure imposed upon it to investigate the faults in the class, in the school, in the rejecting children, in the homeroom teacher, or in the rejected child. The public condemns these actions and punishes the abusive, cruel children, while treating the abused children, sometimes firing the homeroom teacher or even the school principal. All the parties involved – parents, teachers, principals, educational counselors, and educational psychologists – feel that the social problems are beyond their abilities, and that all their interventions and therapies are unable to suppress the severe social phenomena.

In this book, I will present a completely new approach, whose exposure arouses immediate opposition since it requires an absolute change of direction of thinking and understanding regarding this age, with its various phenomena. In order to clarify the approach presented here, let's start with two examples from the early developmental stages in which we'll see how understanding the developmental stage's unique developmental need changes the adults' behavior.

The first example is from the developmental stage of age 2 1/2. At this age, children are possessive. They sense, perceive, feel, and want everything to be only their own. Games, toys, candy, mom and dad, everything is theirs and only theirs. Children at this age become angry if another child takes "their" swing at the public playground. Adults who lack developmental knowledge and do not understand the developmental importance of this "possessiveness" may react with anxiety that their child has an innate quality of extreme possessiveness and is unable to share with others. In response, they may fight this developmental need, demand that their child share with others, and dismiss their child's statement, saying, "No! This swing is not only yours!", and so on. Through their good intention to raise their child to be a beneficial member of society, they can actually harm his or her development.

The second example: 2-year-old children react stubbornly – "I want", "I don't want". These are normative developmental reactions that are important for this age (Raphael-Leff, 2012). Without knowing and understanding the developmental need, parents may mistakenly perceive their child's strong will as a sign of a tyrannical personality, and their anxiety may make them fight their child's will, divert or suppress it, and here too, their good intentions may eventually harm their child's development.

Children's behavior during latency awakens opposition in adults and a strong desire to fight children's "cruelty" and strict social norms, and to automatically go to the aid of the rejected child. But as in the previous examples, such a fight could harm the development of the children during their latency stage. As adults, we must understand that latency is an important developmental stage in which children have a developmental need that we must understand and help to fulfill in order to allow the children to continue to grow and develop.

The approach presented in this book, following my previous book, *Socially Rejected Children* (Fisher-Grafy, 2015), is as follows:

The school is the most significant environmental setting at this stage. It provides the conditions for optimal development for children at the stage where they require nourishment of their social need. The selfobject that provides this nourishment is, usually, the society of classmates. The teachers and parents continue to be the selfobject that provides the children's basic needs, those related to the earlier stages of development. During latency, fulfilling these needs is relegated to the back burner, from which they move onto nourishing the selfobject of their classmates.

The social need is the most significant at this age, and the children's entire essence is focused on fulfilling this need. Social rejection is an inherent, vital, and important part of psychic development at this stage. This will be explained later.

The practical implications of this approach:

• The cruelty in social phenomena during latency is essential, has developmental significance, and does not necessarily indicate the personality or moral level of particular children. All the children involved in social rejection can develop morally and become good and pro-social people in adult life.

• The developmental stage at this age, with all its "cruelty", has great importance for moral development.

• Social rejection shouldn't be fought; it serves the developmental stage.

• The difficulties, flaws, and moral distortion of children shouldn't be treated. The children are acting exactly as expected of them in the current developmental stage.

• The education system, the parents, and the children shouldn't be blamed. Nobody is to blame, and instead a different understanding should arise, requiring a different treatment. When teachers receive knowledge and tools, they can work in accordance with the children and their needs, so that the children will be satisfied and the teachers will also feel fulfilled from bringing the children to this good state.

• Children undergoing a developmental stage during latency should be supported. The responsible adults, meaning the teachers and parents, should have the right position in accordance to the needs of the latency stage so they can help fulfill the essential social needs.

In this book, I shall present the understanding that during elementary school (grades two to five), the age that the psychoanalytical literature terms "the latency stage", a significant psychic development occurs. We must get to know the characteristics and needs of this developmental stage and understand how social rejection serves it. In the second part of the book, I will present a therapy method for socially rejected children. This is the "envelope method", in which children can, already after the first therapy session, make a rapid, immediate change in their social situation. The third part will discuss the school class aspect. Classes in elementary school should be managed as social classes, in which social rejection continues to exist as a significant factor in development. I will present the way the system should operate so that children receive the appropriate response to their developmental need, without deploying social rejection, thus preventing or at least significantly reducing its harmful force and severity. I will also present the school difficulties arising at this age, such as: violating the homeroom teacher's authority and "negative" class norms and provide tools – on the basis of the developmental understanding – for handling them. The fourth part will present an overall educational approach on the basis of the developmental understanding of latency presented in this book.

The approach presented in this book leads to a new, different educational vision. Even the most innovative programs in the education system, which are in fact more appropriate for the developmental stage and the correct ways of behaving with the children at school (programs based on collaborative learning, using online study software, "conversation circles", and so on) are focused on the purpose of teaching the children: how to successfully teach the children in the most efficient and fertile way. The educational approach presented here, in contrast, is of the opinion that children at this stage are undergoing important development, where children must establish an autonomous society of children, and that only in such a society can the individual souls of the children develop properly. Therefore, the focus is not on educating for moral values or academic achievements, but on creating an environment in the school in which the society of children forms an autonomous society with its own dynamics and characteristics, to be described in Chapter 6 and that learning is indeed part of this, but it's not based on the study topics that adults consider appropriate, but on those that the society of children is curious about.

References

Binstock, O. (2003). *The Phenomenological Aspect of Social Rejection by Peers among Socially Normal Students in Elementary and Junior High School*. Ph.D. Dissertation. Jerusalem: Hebrew University [Hebrew].

Fisher-Grafy, H. (2015). *Socially Rejected Children*. Tel Aviv: Resling [Hebrew].

Raphael-Leff, J. (2012). "Terrible twos" and "terrible teens": The importance of play. *Journal of Infant, Child, and Adolescent Psychology*, 11(4): 299–315.

1 Characteristics of "cruelty" during latency

Emotion – where is the emotion?

In my experience, patients during the latency stage who are socially rejected don't cry. Even when they tell me about the most serious harm their classmates caused them, they don't cry. Almost all children, with some exceptions, describe the harm they suffer in a dry, laconic manner. On the other hand, the rejecting children who cause pain to the rejected children don't express any remorse or guilt during the latency stage. They don't have a bad conscience or feel shame about what they did. One boy came to me in a very serious state of social rejection. His rejection was so severe that when he described it, he wrote a list of the hierarchy of all the boys in the class, with him appearing last in the list. After improving his social status using the "envelope method", he got close to the social leaders and became one of them, and at some stage even led the social rejection of another boy in the class. When I tried to awaken his empathy toward the suffering of the rejected boy and to remind him of how he had felt just the month before, he seemed to become completely impervious and there was no opening, not even a small crack, through which I could make him listen to me and arouse even a drop of empathy and compassion.

It's obvious that children during the latency stage are not coldhearted or emotionless. As I learned from my adolescent patients, the same children, a few years later, during adolescence (Hughes et al., 2016), feel severe guilt for their actions during latency. They ask themselves: How could I have treated that boy that way? How could I have been so insensitive? How could I have lacked consideration for the weak? Avoided helping them? In addition to the feelings of guilt and damage to their self-image, they feel regret and hurt for the harm they caused. They don't know how to contain their heartless behavior. I have often heard adults looking back on the stage of their latency age and wondering aloud how they could have behaved like that, and how to contain this episode of their lives when they are now very moral adults, full of consideration for others, who couldn't harm others.

All children during latency are hurt by social rejection

It appears to adults, parents, and teachers that only the socially rejected children suffer from social rejection. In my experience, all the children in the class suffer from the experience of social rejection, and that everyone, without exception, is under constant social pressure. Even children who don't participate at all in the serious social moves, who are passive and avoid taking part in the social harm, bear a heavy burden in adulthood, just like those post-traumatic children who were not harmed themselves but were exposed to family violence.

I have seen several couples, parents of socially rejected children, who told me that when they were the same age as their children in elementary school, they were popular and didn't suffer from social difficulties, but this experience that happened to another child in their class deterred them so much and fixated such a terrible threat in their souls that they raised their own child with constant fear of rejection, and in the end what they had feared actually happened.

It seems to parents and teachers that some children are immune to the social harm of social rejection. There is a tendency to believe that the class king, the class queen, and the popular children in the class don't suffer, that they're protected, stronger than the social forces around them. Adults and children are convinced that the popular children and the class rulers are those who determine the character of the social harm and that they don't have to deal with the social stresses and pressures that the "unpopular" and "rejected" children do, and that they are never hurt. However, in conversations with former class kings and queens, bitter memories arise of severe social behavior directed at them. A large proportion of their classmates fight against them, on various occasions show them contempt, harass them, and don't accept their high place in the hierarchy. In addition, due to their great social power, they often experience a hostile attitude from the teachers as well.

From my experience, I can conclude that all the children in the class absorb the experiences of social rejection and are affected by them.

Expanding circles of cruelty

Inequality – status hierarchy

The cruelty is not only expressed in the difficult social status of the socially rejected children. The whole social perception during the latency stage is founded on inequality and on harming individual rights. The mental development of young children makes them capable of making comparisons. Children aged 5 or 6 express displeasure when they see other children receiving more than them (Sroufe, Cooper, & DeHart, 1996). Children show great sensitivity to equality and are hurt when others are given more than they are given. During latency, this mature mental ability stands in contrast with the social reality in their class. The mental and moral maturity to demand equality is accompanied by the understanding that something is starting to change in the class hierarchy. A group of children becomes strong and dominant, controls the class, becomes a closed group that doesn't make friends with other children, and it's impossible to enter it even with the mediation of parents and teachers. Each child's status becomes obvious and clear. The injustice in the distribution of resources and the inequality between the children are really blatant.

All the children I spoke with knew how to describe the hierarchy with precision, from the class king or queen to the lowest ranked. One of the children, a particularly gifted and creative boy, described the hierarchy as follows: there's an emperor, who is king of the class. Below him are the senators, who make most of the decisions. Their opinion is binding even for the emperor. He listens to them. Below them are the soldiers, who listen to the senators, and the king/emperor hardly has any right to decide about them. Below all these are the simple people, the slaves, who are isolated from society, and whom society doesn't like very much. In parallel to this order, this boy told me, there is also a ranking based exclusively on the ability to play soccer (or any other group sport the boys play). In the top place here is the emperor, who is the best player, and this is not necessarily the class king. Below him are the senators and soldiers, the same children as in the previous hierarchy, and the simple people and slaves are those who don't participate in the game at all.

In a short time, from entering the latency stage until its end, the children are subject to an insufferable reality that contradicts all the values of Western society, including: the aim for equality and the war against prejudice and discrimination for reasons of gender, race, and class. Human society is established on moral values, such as: love thy neighbor like thyself, shaming others in public is equivalent to bloodshed, those who respect others are respected, and so on. The social reality during latency contrasts with these moral values and the democratic values of justice and equality. The social hierarchy at this age determines that some children are important and valued while others aren't (Östberg, 2003).

The important and valued children receive privileges and preferential treatment. Love, admiration, and empathy are only directed at the class rulers and the popular children. Rejected children in the class don't receive such treatment. Often, socially rejected children say that when they propose a game, nobody listens, but when a "popular" child suggests it, everyone listens and wants to play his or her game.

One girl, who was socially rejected and who broke her leg just before a school trip, limped all through the trip with her leg in a cast and dragged behind on her own, without any of the other girls taking any interest in her or showing any gesture of understanding or consideration. In contrast, the popular children receive an empathic response even for the most minor things. When the class queen is upset about a broken pencil tip, all the girls, like a school of fishes, gather around her and show sensitivity, offer help, while heaping on affection, compensation, encouragement, and comfort.

Children at this age accept the hierarchy and the inequality as the law of the world. They accept it as the one and only reality, which can't be changed. All fourth and fifth grades have a class king or class queen; every class has popular and unpopular children. This division is unchangeable. It occurs as part of the developmental stage and is inherent for the intrapsychic development, as will be explained later.

One day, the children awaken to the internal and external reality of a social hierarchy. It happens by itself, without the children doing anything deliberate to create it. Even though they are all capable of comparing and knowing that there are those with privileges and those who are disadvantaged, they don't fight it. They cooperate and even take it for granted. Not so the rejected children. They refuse to accept the inequality. Many children argue: why should I treat him (the class king) or her (the class queen) in a certain way if he or she doesn't treat me that way? Why should I give her something of mine when she doesn't give me something of hers? Other socially rejected girls say that the empathic treatment of the class queen is "fake". The girls don't really pity the class queen. The important point is the following oxymoron: the socially rejected children are not rejected due to the social hierarchy that marginalizes them. They are rejected precisely because they fight and are unwilling to accept the reality in which a clear and explicit social hierarchy exists.

The destructive implications of children's cruelty

The destructive implications of the cruelty entailed in social rejection for the children's futures have been found and confirmed in many studies. The damage of social rejection is found in the present and the future, in all areas of functioning: health (Einsenberg et al., 2014); behavior (McDougall et al., 2001); education (Benner & Graham, 2013); and emotion (Greene, Way, & Pahl, 2006). Other findings include phenomena of criminality, crime, and psychopathology in adulthood (Reijntjes et al., 2011), and damage to professional development, employment status, satisfaction with social connections, and insecurity in forming romantic attachments during adulthood (Ashton, 2006). My impression is that the harmful implications are extensive and profound. I argue that the harm during latency influences the majority of children, and the depth of the harm touches upon essential layers of self-image and self-esteem. Studies have yet to be conducted on this issue, but from my experience, most of the latency age children in the class are "unpopular" children. In an average class, I estimate that about a third of the classmates are "popular". Some other children are socially rejected, and the vast majority of the class's children are "unpopular". They will experience the label of being "unpopular" for most of their years in elementary school. For three or four years of the latency stage, every day they experience sensations of lack of popularity and unequal treatment. They experience a reality where other children are worth more than them. Often, the overt excuse given for this by the society of classmates is very frustrating, because it isn't related to the rejected children themselves or their skills or behavior. For example, an unpopular boy was rejected from soccer games due to physical clumsiness and often humiliated for this. Or a girl rejected by the popular girls due to her low socio-economic status. The children give their rejection overt reasons, external to the rejected children, that don't depend on them, their personality, or their behavior, and this is very difficult for the rejected children. The feeling that there's something that doesn't depend upon me that determines my fate, that I can't change, fixates a sense of low self-esteem along with great frustration due to the injustice and the inability to change. In practice, the external factors given to explain the unpopularity are not the source and origin of this feeling, as will be explained later.

Children can change their status. As we'll see later on, the power and control are in their hands. The reason isn't external to the children, though it is related to their developmental progress. The natural experience, common at this age, places the blame for unpopularity or rejection on some external factor that doesn't depend on them and their behavior and is therefore unchangeable. According to the perception of latency age children, they receive treatment that doesn't take them and their desires into account. The unpopular children feel inferior to the others. They don't receive appreciation, admiration, and belonging the way the popular children do. They are not sought after by them; they don't receive empathy and understanding like the popular children. To their great frustration, they are transparent in the eyes of their classmates, unimportant, invisible, and unheard. The discriminatory attitude comes in addition to the terrible knowledge that this bad treatment indicates, unfortunately, their low status. Throughout the years of elementary school, most children in the class experience themselves in the horrible way described here. The low self-esteem of the unpopular children is based on their inferior status and on what this implies for their value in the eyes of others. Thus, during latency, when the self-image and self-esteem are formed mainly around the company of classmates, for most of the years of elementary school, most children in the class form low self-image and self-esteem.

The situation of the socially rejected children is much worse. In addition to what we described about the "unpopular" children, there are hard feelings of rejection, not belonging, and the worst damage is the cessation of psychic development. They observe from the sidelines the social lives, events, conversations, games, and social activities of their classmates, feeling that this is where real life happens. Where the popular children are, a vivid, dynamic social life occurs. That's where the significant psychic life exists, while they, the rejected children, are not there, not part of it. Their psyche doesn't continue to develop in the natural developmental environment of this stage – the society of children.

Let's collect the four features mentioned so far: lack of emotion; hierarchy and inequality; all children suffering from social rejection; most children suffering from low self-image and low self-esteem. We can ask: What is actually happening during latency? Why is cruelty so widespread at this age? We see that the children can act cruelly during social rejection, without the active presence of feelings of empathy and morality. We also see that the cruelty is not just in the children's behavior, but that the entire social reality of social hierarchy and status inequality happens universally in all societies of children in a natural developmental manner. Also, we identify severe damage to self-image and self-esteem. This damage is common to almost all children: rejected, unpopular, but also the popular children and class rulers. Even those who seem not to share the damage experience the social trauma passively and may even transfer it onto their own children.

So, how can we explain this cruelty, which we have seen is extensive and encompasses all the children at this stage? The hierarchy that starts to exist in the class naturally, the social status, the inequality, the manipulative feelings, the lack of empathy and emotion? How can we explain the extensive phenomenon that occurs at this age, that a society of children treats each other with injustice and inequality, often with an insulting, humiliating, and cruel attitude, without emotion and empathy, with none of the children daring to condemn and stop these phenomena, and when one righteous person does, he or she is sentenced to a severe social response? Is the inclination of the human heart evil from his youth? Do we naturally have the morality of *Lord of the Flies*, living according to the cold rules of the jungle, man to man is a wolf? After all, the phenomena common during latency can also be seen in adulthood, in the relations between groups, when one group treats another group immorally.

In their chapter on group morality, Leach, Bilali, and Pagliaro (2015) asked this question about general morality. The chapter's conclusion states that morality is a group phenomenon in which an oxymoron exists whereby morally trampling an out-group relieves the group members of personal morality. Individual immoral behavior has been found in a range of famous social psychology experiments. For example, Milgram's experiment in 1962, Zimbardo's prison experiment, and Asch's experiment testing group conformity. Is this our true nature, and do we become good people only through education? If this is true, those who accuse teachers and parents of faulty education are right. But just a moment, we are born with the capacity for morality, and children's morality develops, as studies have found. Developmental research has found that babies have an internal moral basis, the ability and willingness to judge the actions of strangers, a preliminary sense of justice, and an intuitive response to evil (Holvoet et al., 2016). Other studies show that already at an early age, children have abilities related to moral judgment (Zhang et al., 2013) and that pro-social behavior exists in the early stages of development (Dunfield & Kuhlmeier, 2013). If so, how can we explain these failings in morality? Where does the innate moral capacity, which develops during early childhood, go during latency? How can we explain that immediately at the end of latency, in early adolescence, the good morality returns in full, and the social phenomena of injustice, inequality, and discrimination for reasons of gender, race, nationality, religion, or group are morally condemned?

References

Ashton, P.T. (2006). Middle childhood: Period of latency or context of development? [Review of the book *Developmental Contexts in Middle Childhood: Bridges to Adolescence and Adulthood*, edited by A.C. Huston & M.N. Ripke]. *PsycCRITIQUES*, 51(39).

Benner, A.D. & Graham, S. (2013). The antecedents and consequences of racial/ethnic discrimination during adolescence: Does the source of discrimination matter? *Developmental Psychology*, 49(8): 1602–1613.

Dunfield, K.A. & Kuhlmeier, V.A. (2013). Classifying prosocial behavior: Children's responses to instrumental need, emotional distress, and material desire. *Child Development*, 84: 1766–1776.

Eisenberg, N., Spinrad, T.L., & Morris, A.S. (2014). Empathy-related responding in children. In *Handbook of Moral Development*, edited by M. Killen & J.G. Smetana (pp. 184–207). New York: Psychology Press.

Greene, M.L., Way, N., & Pahl, K. (2006). Trajectories of perceived adult and peer discrimination among Black, Latino, and Asian American adolescents: Patterns and psychological correlates. *Developmental Psychology*, 42(2): 218–236.

Holvoet, C., Scola, C., Arciszewski, T., & Picard, D. (2016). Infants' preference for prosocial behaviors: A literature review. *Infant Behavior & Development*, 45(Part B): 125–139.

Hughes, D., Del, T.J., Harding, J., Way, N., & Rarick, J. (2016). Trajectories of discrimination across adolescence: Associations with academic, psychological and behavioral outcomes. *Child Development*, 87: 1337–1351.

Leach, C.W., Bilali, R., & Pagliaro, S. (2015). Groups and morality. In *APA Handbook of Personality and Social Psychology*, Vol. 2. *Group Processes*, edited by J. Simpson & J.F. Dovidio. Washington, DC: American Psychological Association.

McDougall, P., Hymel, S., Vaillancourt, T., & Mercer, L. (2001). The consequences of early childhood rejection. In *Interpersonal Rejection*, edited by M. Leary (pp. 213–247). New York: Oxford University Press.

Östberg, V. (2003). Children in classrooms: Peer status, status distribution, and mental well-being. *Social Science and Medicine*, 56(1): 17–29.

Reijntjes, A., Thomaes, S., Boelen, P., van der Schoot, M., de Castro, B.O., & Telch, M. (2011). Delighted when approved by others, to pieces when rejected: Children's social anxiety magnifies the linkage between self- and other-evaluations. *Journal of Child Psychology Psychiatry*, 52(7): 774–781.

Sroufe, L.A., Cooper, R.G., & DeHart, G.B. (1996). *Child Development: Its Nature Course*. Boston: McGraw Hill.

Zhang, A., Dong, N.-J., Li, Y., & Tzu-Jung, M. (2013). Children's moral reasoning: Influence of culture and collaborative discussion. *Journal of Cognition and Culture*, 13(5): 503–522.

2 Social rejection

Social rejection: review of literature and therapy

Psychological research has focused on social rejection during latency mainly from two perspectives. Most studies attempt to find psychopathology factors and personality qualities in the rejected children or their parents. A few studies have examined the role of group processes in social rejection among children (Rutland & Killen, 2017). In recent years, the Social Reasoning Developmental (SRD) approach has offered a new research direction, studying the processes of making a moral decision in the intra-group context. Studies employing this approach focus on three factors that are involved in making moral decisions within groups: morality (fairness, equality, and rights); group processes (group identity, group norms, and hierarchical status); and a psychological perspective of the self and others (independence and knowledge of the other's mental state) (Rutland & Killen, 2015).

These research avenues, surprisingly, don't take into consideration the following facts:

- Studies indicate a reduction in children's morality, particularly during latency. Thus, for instance, a long-term study examining the frequency of pro-social behaviors of latency age children (showing sympathy, praising others, assisting sick or injured children, helping in difficult tasks, inviting others to join a game, intervening to end arguments, helping others tidy and collect items, consoling sad children) found that the frequency of pro-social behaviors doesn't increase between the ages of 10 and 15, and according to teachers' reports, even declines (Nantel-Vivier et al., 2009), and then increases again during adolescence (Hughes et al., 2016).
- In contrast to the studies that found disabilities and psychopathology among the rejected children and their parents, other studies reject these findings. In my experience, almost all of the rejected children

are capable, talented, attractive, athletic, and perceptive, and they fully understand the social map. Also, most of the parents of the socially rejected children are deeply involved in raising their children, full of love and concern.

• Group processes in classes that influence all groups in the same way are not necessarily related to group processes that are specific to a particular group. However, the group processes in all classes are similar, and they all lead to social rejection. Therefore, there must be some factor that mandates them, which awakens them precisely during latency. These processes are universal, and therefore they must be developmental.

The connection between psychological research and treating social rejection

At present, two methods of treating social rejection are common, and they suit the two research directions: intervening in the class dynamics as the main creator of the rejection phenomenon (Greene et al., 2016) and Cognitive-Behavioral Therapy (Zimmer-Gembeck et al., 2016) for the psychopathology and personality difficulties of the rejected child. Therapy for the rejected children, whether using long-term dynamic Cognitive-Behavioral Therapy or in group therapy for social skills, focuses on correcting the rejected child's disability, difficulties, and sensitivity. The rejected children's experience is: first, being victims of social injustice; and in the second stage, the experience of treating their faults, offered in the form of tools for correcting social skills. In my opinion, as if it were not enough for the children to be humiliated in their class, now in therapy they are presented as having difficulties, sensitivity, or a disability. The finger of blame, even if covert and unexpressed, is directed at the children and their inability to fit in properly.

The finger of blame is also directed, harmfully, at other parties. It is aimed just as forcefully at the educators. It is mainly the teachers who are blamed and considered responsible for the faults and difficulties in the class dynamics. This responsibility is ascribed to them by the parents and the education system. The accused teachers operate in various ways to overcome the phenomenon. Sometimes they go to battle and fight against the society of children, the hierarchy, the class rulers, and the children's "negative" norms. Sometimes they raise the power of education, teaching with an iron fist, enhancing the children's values, empathy, and guilt feelings. Thus, a teacher can pontificate emotionally to the children, or hurl accusations at them: How could they treat a child so negatively? Don't they know he is suffering and that this hurts him very much? How would they feel if they were treated that way? The teachers' lack of tools and their frustration can lead them to hurt, offend, or punish the class and the rejecting children. Since the system blames the teacher, teachers redouble their efforts: they try to persuade the class rulers to change the processes and atmosphere in the class; they search for at least one good friend for the rejected child and make efforts to bring the two together. They empower the rejected children, emphasizing their talents, giving them roles that place them in the spotlight. They persuade the "unpopular" and rejected children that they should make friends with other "unpopular" children. They empower a group of "good" children who are not popular to become a counter-group to be strengthened and to overcome the group of popular children, who behave "negatively". They often adopt a strategy whereby they encourage the rejected children to fight back: "Stand up for yourself!"; "Don't give in to them!". They even encourage the children to approach them about any problematic social matter and even to inform on children who hurt them. They often involve the parents. In general, they fight the children's cruel values. If only they knew that this was not the children's fault, that the developmental element involved must be recognized, and that not only do these actions by the teachers not help, they actually operate in the precise opposite direction from a developmental perspective.

Social rejection as part of a developmental stage

Something happens during latency. Things start to change. From the second grade onward, clear lines start forming that are different from those in earlier developmental stages. Let's present the developmental characteristics of the latency stage:

Reduction in the exclusivity of parents and educators

In kindergarten and first grade, children grant significant exclusive importance to the kindergarten teacher and the homeroom teacher, similar to that given to parents. From second grade onward, throughout latency, the society of children gains importance. As part of the separation process, the children separate from the first attachment figures (parents and teachers) and move over to the society of children in the class (Shustorovich & Weinstein, 2010), which becomes most significant during latency. The society of children determines the children's internal feelings, mental wellbeing, language, speech, and also behavior: walking gait, clothing style, playing mode, and favorite games. When there's a clash between the teacher's authority and the class's social power, the children often demonstrate external respect to the adult authority figure, but under the surface they act in accordance with the dictates of the society of children.

Young children appeal to significant adults for help with their difficulties. Children who are mature during latency tend not to approach their parents and teachers. They will manage on their own, within the society of children in their class. Children who are not mature during latency continue to stick to their parents as significant figures. For example, a fourth-grade girl who says: "I must tell mom and dad everything" or "I can't do this, it's against my parents' wishes". Other children are not released by their parents, who continue to dominate their lives. For example: a mother and daughter came to an appointment with me, and the mother came into the room with her daughter, then accompanied her to the bathroom and waited outside until she finished. The mother told me that she fought with the teachers for her daughter's grades and was active in the PTA. Children who are immature during latency prefer to appeal to the teachers as the chief authority in managing their social lives: "Miss, they didn't include me", or "Miss, punish them!". Immature children sometimes ask their parents to intervene in their social difficulties and even encourage the parents to speak to the homeroom teacher or to the parents of children who mistreat them. They obey teachers who invite the children to complain about social difficulties, blame other children, and expect the homeroom teacher to punish them. They are often considered as informants and as babyish. The society of children doesn't show them any tolerance and often punishes them through severe social rejection. These children don't match their developmental stage, in which the significant development context is that of the society of classmates rather than the figures of parents and teachers. Studies have found that the academic and behavioral functioning during latency and the continued professional and social development during adulthood clearly depend on one main variable during middle childhood: social integration (Ashton, 2006). The importance of parental care and family quality are not as significant as the society of children at this age.

Reduction in egocentricity, grandiosity, object control, and omnipotence

Established psychological theories describe babies and infants as subject to an internal reality that is not bound by the laws of real external reality. Children will exist in the egocentric function of "I" and frequently say "I want it!" and "I like it!" (Bartsch & Wellman, 1995). Children will be angry when they are prevented from achieving their goals (Hofmann & Doan, 2018). Significant figures shape their emotions (Malatesta et al., 1989). They perceive infants as seeing themselves as the center of the world: "His Majesty the Baby" (Freud, 1914: 91) and "the centre of the universe" (Winnicott, 1951/1958). The events and circumstances of the world are connected to them. This egocentric position doesn't take into account additional perspectives, and thus children find it difficult to delay personal gratification in the face of the limitations of reality. Infants expect their needs and desires to be fulfilled, always. Thus, when their needs are fulfilled, this strengthens their omnipotence (Winnicott, 1951/1958) and their need to feel that they control the object (mother, father). The proper development during the early years occurs when the needs for grandiosity, egocentrism, and omnipotence are satisfied during a process of separation from the objects who grant the needs. According to the Object Relations approach, during the process of separation and individuation, the infantile grandiosity, exhibitionism, and omnipotence are reduced (Mahler, 1975).

According to Kohut (1971), the process of separation between children and their key objects crystalizes and stabilizes the system of regulating self-value. Kohut explains that when the self and the object become distinct from each other, grandiosity is transformed into self-value through the internal regulation of handling failures and stress situations. For example, a delay in the described development causes children to find it difficult to accept losing a game. The sight of children crying with frustration and stopping a game in the middle with tears of rage because they lost is common during the early years. Children are unable to accept that someone won who wasn't them. That someone has a superior position that isn't theirs. From latency, children are able to accept situations of losing.

Mark, an attractive and smart third-grade boy, is perceived by his mother as having many problems, and many appointments with the parents revolved around his emotional and social difficulties. In therapy, he built a whole city out of wooden blocks and named it "Mark City", with Mark streets, Mark highways, Mark signs, Mark department stores, Mark cars, and Mark people. He was the omnipotent ruler of Mark City. The subjects were his slaves. He had infinite money and power. People behaved only according to his wishes, and of course everyone obeyed him. Outside therapy, in the company of children at school, he manipulated the children in a sophisticated manner, through a game where the losers became his servants.

From the second and third grade, egocentricity and omnipotence are not reduced according to the paradigm presented here, and remain fully powerful but blocked within the self core. These primary needs remain fully powerful throughout life, but during latency they are blocked and controlled in the social self cytoplasm through cognitive-realistic means. In latency, children live a new internal psychic reality. In this reality, there is no "one true self", but a consciousness of our self in the minds of others (Schilbach et al., 2008). From an emotional point of view, the complex ability to understand mixed emotions that didn't exist up to the end of the Oedipal stage emerges during latency (Harter & Buddin, 1987). The self transitions from a physical being with individual thoughts and needs to a social being that conforms with social norms (Selman & Byrne, 1974). In this reality, the society of children is the center of the world, reality doesn't behave according to their own wishes, and they are not its sole rulers. This reality contains rules that are essentially different from the children's individual rules, and above all, there is now a society of children that has needs and desires that differ from those of the individual children. Latency age children don't feel omnipotent, grandiose, and egocentric. Instead, they feel "amazing", valuable, and confident when they are socially popular. Children who continue demanding from the society of children and from their teachers affirmation of their grandiosity and omnipotence; who want to receive approval from their teacher; who help the teacher in order to receive praise; who don't flow with the society of children into behaviors the teachers don't accept; who seek out the spotlight to position themselves as best and most successful (such as the teacher saying to the class: "Kids, look at Brad, he's such a good boy") – these children will be unanimously rejected by the society of children.

Popularity and social rejection

Studies have tried to link popularity, unpopularity, and social rejection to external factors such as: athletic ability, external appearance, socio-economic status, and so on. I argue that being popular children during latency doesn't depend on appearance, physical strength, sporting achievements, the ability to play soccer or basketball, high academic achievements, special talents, or socio-economic status. Being socially popular doesn't depend on race or religion. Aggressive boys won't necessarily be socially rejected, and pro-social, polite, socially skilled, helpful, cooperative, and considerate girls won't necessarily be popular. For example, a fourth-grade girl told me that she always gives the other girls whatever they ask, but when she asks for something, none of them gives it to her. She told me of a case where she had just given another girl a pencil sharpener, and then she asked the same girl for an eraser, and this girl refused to give her something of her own. I asked: "How do the popular girls behave? Do they give each other things?" She replied: "They never give anything and never help". If so, I told her, you have to behave like them. "What? Not to give them anything?" I nodded. "I don't believe this. What would my parents think of me? They are educating me to be helpful. What would my teacher think of me? I can't be a bad girl in their eyes". Children have a need to be "like everyone else" in order to be accepted socially (Over & Carpenter, 2013).

In order to be popular, to feel that the society of children appreciates and accepts them, children must act like everyone else. Up to the age of 6 to 7, children receive approval and appreciation from adults for demonstrating unique and exclusive talents. During latency, in contrast, children receive approval, appreciation, and popularity for being prominent in the commonly agreed social realm. Prominence is in being the best at being similar to everyone else. For example, if a society of boys in the class prefer playing soccer rather than basketball, a boy who's good at basketball won't be considered popular. A boy who's good at soccer will be considered popular. Even within the game of soccer, there are small nuances that require children to be like everyone else. The hierarchy isn't determined only by each boy's control of the ball and ability to score goals. Even in soccer, there are norms the boys have to follow. Those who disobey are rejected. For example, they aren't allowed to kick to the goal unless the rest of the boys approve. Boys who kick on their own initiative, even if they score goals, won't receive approval and may even be rejected and humiliated. Or the "king" of the boys could hand out roles for defense and offense and the boys must accept his decisions. Obeying the verbal and non-verbal rules is what guarantees acceptance. When boys can't kick accurately but still act in accordance with what the boys have agreed, the society of boys will forgive the failure. Another example: the girls in the class wear a certain type of leggings. When a girl shows up in class wearing a different, special, and expensive pair of leggings, she might be instantly rejected. In contrast, a girl who buys leggings that are exactly identical to all the absolute details the girls have agreed upon will get wonderful positive feedback.

If so, social popularity is not based on external factors unrelated to the children, their behavior, and their abilities. A girl who is rejected because her family isn't wealthy or a boy who is rejected just because he's no good at soccer – these are external reasons the children choose to blame, when the reasons for acceptance and popularity are actually related to the social system and social norms. The children's own behavior is what determines their unpopular social status, by demonstrating their high skills and abilities and becoming prominent as a solo player above the rest. It's precisely by demonstrating their ability to accept what is normal and agreed in the society of classmates and to behave closely and similarly to the society of children that they will gain acceptance.

An increase in the ability to delay gratification, in restraint, self-control, and regulation

Young children, along with their egocentricity, omnipotence, and grandiosity, expect their desires to be fulfilled immediately. Babies exist with a basic and absolute certainty that when they wish to nurse, their desire is fulfilled instantly as if by magic. Two-year-olds expect and feel certain that their desires, even if sometimes delayed, will be fulfilled. When they don't receive attention, they can cry with frustration. Children aged 5–6 can already respond to the requirement for restraint and self-control but may sometimes still respond with great frustration. When they are disappointed by their desires not being fulfilled, for example, when their friends don't do what they want, they can respond with tears, aggression, and violence. During latency, strong personal desire and object control don't disappear or diminish. Developed realistic mental abilities don't detract from the desire and the need for control. In latency, personal desire and object control are naturally blocked, while the desire of the society of classmates and its control over the children's behavior become dominant. Latency age children accept naturally, without any conflict, a reality in which their desires aren't automatically accepted or are greatly delayed, or that the society of children has different desires and preferences, or rules that don't allow their wishes to be realized, at least not immediately. Mature latency age children don't feel there is a clash between their own wishes and the will of the group because they feel that group's will is their personal will while they function in the social self. This is in contrast with younger children, who express their frustration in a physical-sensory way, crying or hitting. Latency age children don't express any frustration when their will isn't realized. Accordingly, the society of children supports this development by not tolerating children who can't control their emotions in situations of rivalry, frustration, and failure, who respond in a childish, physical manner through crying, violence, or appealing to a significant adult for help. When children insist upon their personal desire, fight, and reject the group's will, the group doesn't permit this.

Defense mechanisms

Theoreticians have emphasized the importance of defense mechanisms as a central feature of development during latency (Sarnoff, 1976; Becker, 1974; Kaplan, 1965). Anna Freud (1936) argued that during latency, all the defense mechanisms already exist. According to her, the defense mechanisms enable children to control their urges and internal desires and to handle the requirements of external reality better. Rapaport (1967) presented the autonomous quality of the defense mechanisms and their double role during latency. In his opinion, the defense mechanisms are not those that exist during the Oedipal stage, where they originate from instinctive sources. The defense mechanisms during latency are essentially different. They are autonomous and deal with the external environment that exists at this age. Sarnoff (1976) sees children's egos during latency as different from adults' egos, especially in their age group, their contents, the conformity, and the intensity of several defense mechanisms whose role is to deal with the outbursts of urges from the previous stages: anal, genital, and the Oedipal conflict. To conclude, the theoreticians share a common attribution of a double role to the defense mechanisms. On the one hand, handling intrapsychic conflicts, urges, and internal desires, and on the other hand, dealing with external reality.

The development of defense mechanisms has great importance during the latency developmental stage. According to the developmental paradigm presented in detail in the next chapter, they are important because during latency they exist in full and are formed within a part of the self, in a sort of "membrane", which blocks the infantile being: egocentricity, grandiosity, omnipotence. This part enables the transition to the new part of the self that awakens during latency, in which children exist in a very particular social psychic reality.

Intrapsychic and extrapsychic formation

Erikson (1950) argues that prior to latency, there is a bi-directional psychic development: first, turning inward to form the self-image, and second, turning outward toward social expansion. According to Erikson and others, the central developmental feature of latency is the distinction between outside and inside. Children have internal desires, but outwardly they behave in ways that take reality into consideration. Children understand that like them, others are also not necessarily acting according to their internal feeling. Children start to learn how to treat others, who also have an overt side and a covert side. In contrast with the younger ages, in which children speak honestly and state their desires and opinions directly, during latency children start saying things that differ from their true wishes, and sometimes they start lying. Contrary to our tendency as adults to be disappointed by the discovery of lying during latency, at this age lies are actually an indication of normative development of the external, covert part of the self. Children start hiding their thoughts and desires. They start acting according to the requirements of politeness. They operate in the external part of their self, which is directed at society. As I understand it, the authenticity, directness, and honesty typical of the younger age don't disappear. But children during latency exist in an external psychic reality that is different, where they often behave in an intellectual, strategic, manipulative way, due to reasons and considerations of social interests. The hiding, lying, and politeness are not, as many think, the spoiling of the nice qualities of young children. These lies, concealment, and manners are a basic innate psychic experience that awakens during latency. Children don't lie to hide something personal or to adapt themselves to an adult in an accommodating manner. Latency age children live in a social reality in which the expression of intentions and desires is related to the society of children. This necessarily requires them not to express their inner desires, with which they aren't in contact at all during latency.

Interpersonal friendship ("best friends") and group friendships

Children possess two types of motivation: developing social connections that lead them to be loved, and making themselves prominent to lead to popularity. However, while both types motivate them, they usually act on just one of these motivations rather than both (Rodkin et al., 2012). These findings concur with the approaches of Harris (1998) and Sullivan (1953). According to Harris, during latency two social systems exist: one focusing on dyadic relationships, in which pro-social skills develop, such as empathy, listening, understanding others, and helping others (beloved children), while the other focuses on group issues and social popularity (popular children). Harris considers group friendship to be the center of latency age children's being. Sullivan, too, argues that at this age children's need for group belonging takes precedence over their need for individual friendship. According to Sullivan, group popularity in this age group results from developing healthy attitudes toward competition, conformity, and achievements.

Interpersonal friendships among younger children are usually between two children. You can see friendships between two children aged 4 to 6. Usually, children have several interpersonal friendship relationships between two individuals. In other words, each child can have a few close friends, and their relationships are based on a connection between a pair. Often, parents contribute to creating these connections. The two best friends will prefer each other's unique company. While playing at kindergarten or in the first grade, they will play a social game with the same best friend they will meet in the afternoon as well. At any meeting, they will prefer to play with their best friend or two best friends. The essence of interpersonal friendship is: the uniqueness of the attachment, loyalty, commitment, and permanence in the relationship despite changes in the environment.

During second grade, a change occurs. Friendship is a group affair (Sullivan, 1933). The essence of this sort of friendship is different. While the children still call each other "my friend", as they did in kindergarten or the first grade, the fifth-grade friend is different from the friends at younger ages. A kindergarten "friend" is qualitatively unlike a fifth-grade "friend". During the third, fourth, and fifth grades, a friend isn't a best friend. A friend is someone who connects to social status, who belongs to a social stratum, who ensures group membership and popularity. The measure of friendship is popularity and social status. Therefore, children prefer to be friends with popular children, thus raising their social status, which guarantees their popularity and social demand. More children will want to be friends with someone who's popular, and thus that child is in demand and has more friends. The essence of such friendships is: lack of loyalty, lack of permanence in the relationship, and changes in it resulting from changes in the situation and social status.

In the experience of the socially rejected children, their "best friends" from kindergarten and the first or second grade become "traitors", preferring popular friends and avoiding contact with their old "best friend". This behavior is particularly prominent among pairs of best friends when one makes friends with the popular children in the class and the other is rejected by them.

> My best friend is betraying me. He was my best friend last year, but this year he's friends with the popular boys. He ignores me and treats me badly, just like them. He laughs at me, hits me, humiliates me. Only sometimes, in the afternoon, he comes to visit me, but tells me not to tell anyone that he's meeting with me.

Adults, such as parents and teachers, often advise the less popular or rejected children not to remain alone, to have at least one best friend. Parents of socially rejected children may even been alarmed by their children abandoning their previous best friends and preferring to have no friends at all just to get closer to the popular children. They don't understand the essential developmental component and pressure their children to invite their old best friends over in the afternoon. Parents find it hard to accept their children abandoning their good friends, who are fine, quality children, and preferring to get close to the popular children, whom the parents often consider unsuitable. They give their children messages that are opposed to the natural flow of their development.

Stereotypes

During latency, children form basic stereotypes and typical behaviors based on gender: the boys are adventurous, risk-taking, forceful when joining groups, and usually play competitive sports in large groups. They have great physical closeness and little emotional and verbal closeness. They stress loyalty and rank their importance in society based on power, control, leadership, and victory. The girls listen to new members of their group, since they have higher social awareness than the boys. They form intimate relationships that include sharing secrets and mutual support. The girls hang out in small groups, aimed at uniformity and verbal and emotional closeness. Often, talking amongst themselves is the actual activity (Sroufe, Cooper, &

Dehart, 1996). At the ages of 4–6, there are differences in the games of boys and girls (girls: games that simulate families, dolls; boys: moving, constructing, soccer). These differences are natural and serve a personal inner need. Girls set up a dollhouse with their friends, and this satisfies their inner needs. Boys drive objects around in a cart and build fortifications in the sand, and this satisfies some personal inner need. During latency, these differences take on a new quality. They become stereotypes. The stereotypes exist in an inner-psychic social reality.

The great innovation during latency is that the society of children gives the stereotype a specific shape. The template of the stereotype that awakens during latency is filled with content given it by the society of children. Adults, parents, and teachers see stereotypes as a serious problem that should be disputed. Various approaches see stereotypes as the origin of prejudice and discrimination. They don't take into account the developmental benefit of stereotypes. For example, the stereotype of boys this age is related to strength. The meaning of strength changes based on the class and age. In one class, being a strong boy means being an excellent soccer player or computer game player; in another class it could be physical or verbal strength; and in another class strength might be expressed in the ability to be restrained when provoked. In a religious class, the meaning of being strong might be measured in religiosity. Being strong in the society of boys could mean being outstanding in a rare sport or collecting cards from a particular series. Even within the same class, the stereotype of strength can change over time. Boys could fight over strength in a certain computer game, and the next day strength could be expressed in skill in a new sport. The way the stereotypes are expressed can vary between classes and even change at different times. In one class, joining a soccer game requires forceful entry into the game, while in another class, a considerate approach will allow a boy to join the game.

The stereotypes during latency occur in the natural environment. They occur among boys in their natural environment, such as competitive sports in large groups, while for the girls they arise in the subjects of their conversations in small groups, revolving around issues such as: friendship, family, games, fashion, and so on. The boys' stereotype is often presented as having great physical closeness and little emotional and verbal closeness, as stressing loyalty, and as ranking their importance in society according to power, strength, and control. In my experience, there are groups of boys that don't consider the stereotype of boys to include not talking much or being a charismatic leader. I've often noticed that popular boys can be very talkative, or not show any signs of charismatic leadership, quite the opposite: they are flexible and amenable to accepting others' opinions.

The stereotype of girls is commonly presented as having higher social awareness than the boys. They form intimate relationships, which include sharing secrets and mutual support, hanging out in small groups aimed at uniformity and verbal and emotional closeness. Often talking among the group is the activity itself. Here, too, the stereotypes can change. There can be groups of girls who play soccer, or those whose social awareness isn't well developed.

Studies tend to show a connection between social status and stereotypes related to race and religion. Children can be rejected because they don't belong to the right race, nationality, socio-economic status, or religion. Conversely, some children become popular due to having the right race, nationality, or high socio-economic status. In my experience, these stereotypes aren't significant during latency. The significant stereotypes are those that the society of children determines itself and fills with content that is specific to their group. Stereotypes serve the latency age children's psychic development by supporting the social norms and social hierarchy. Children develop during latency by following the contents of the stereotypes in their class. Thus, an example is when they suit the stereotype of being a "strong boy" in a computer game chosen by the society of boys. In a converse, complementary manner, the society of children determines the stereotypes in accordance with the social hierarchy. Popular children could, for example, come from an ethnic group that society generally considers "lower", but in the class they actually have high status, and the class's children aim to adopt the characteristics of that ethnic group. In my experience, children can certainly be "popular" or the "class ruler" when they come from a race, ethnicity, or socio-economic status that the adults consider lower. When there is a stereotype that removes a child from the society of children, he or she can act immediately to return to social belonging by accepting the hierarchy. Thus, for example, boys from a "lower" ethnicity can become socially popular if they become strong in an area that determines the hierarchy, such as soccer. Or girls can become popular if they join in their classmates' excited chatter about a television series. When the "class queen" is proud of an expensive brand item, the other girls in the group show approval and appreciation. Following the social norms and the social hierarchy establishes the children's status without any connection to external characteristics like race, nationality, and so on. Another example: a girl who wanted to fit in with the popular girls, who were all from a high socioeconomic status, can fit in despite not coming from a high socio-economic status home if she makes friends with a popular girl, subordinates herself to the class queen's rule, or ardently sticks to the social norms. Moreover, the girls who are popular on the basis of socio-economic status don't achieve this through examining their families' property, assets, and bank accounts, but through an agreed basis that indicates "prestige". For instance, the girls wear prestigious brand clothing, and it's the society of girls that determines which companies are considered prestigious. These brands the society of girls considers prestigious are often objectively not prestigious at all, but what matters is that the society of girls decides that they are.

Keeping the boundaries between the sexes

Children aged 5 to 6 years may experience a situation where they are "in love" with a child of the opposite sex, and even become a boyfriend and girlfriend pair with them. They sometimes fantasize about marrying this opposite sex child. During latency, boys and girls move apart from each other and a barrier is formed between them (Sroufe, Cooper, & DeHart, 1996). Usually, they don't engage in social contact, don't speak to each other, don't play together, and don't hang out in the same place. A girl who chooses to play soccer with the boys is usually rejected by the girls, and a boy who prefers to spend his break time with the girls will be rejected by the boys. In addition to this separation, there is distancing and avoidance of anything related to sexuality. Latency age children are revolted by anything related to love between the sexes, disgusted by the opposite sex, and not interested in sex. Even the sexual curiosity, the sex games, the investigation of the sexual parts of children of the opposite sex, which were common at age 5 to 6, disappear without a trace. Adults, parents, and teachers see the gender-based distancing and rejection as a difficulty and try to change this. For example, a principal fought this phenomenon through couple dances and competitions during breaks, which raised protests from the children and led to severe intervention by the parents. Another common mistake is when adults encourage a socially rejected, lonely child to play with members of the opposite sex.

Social norms

During kindergarten and first grade, there are no independent social norms. The parents, kindergarten teacher, and homeroom teacher determine the rules and hold the authority. The rules that are dictated are the general social moral rules, the manners of society. Children who argue turn to the kindergarten teacher or homeroom teacher, who judges the situation according to society's accepted values: "Don't hit!", "Don't curse!", "Ask him nicely", "Say you're sorry", "Share!", "If he lets you, you have to let him", "He deserves it too", "It's not nice when one receives a lot and the rest don't", "It's not nice not to share", "Don't swear, it's offensive". Kindergarten teachers and first-grade teachers educate for morality and even succeed at this. Young children are obedient and educated. In normative development, from the second grade onward, changes occur in the children's morality.

Developments in the social and mental abilities occur concurrently with the understanding of and obedience to the class social norms (Hofmann & Doan, 2018). Mature children of latency age obey the society of children and the social norms in their class (Sroufe, Cooper, & DeHart, 1996). These norms are the key for all social behavior. They are the most important foundation for social behavior and they support the intrapsychic development, as will be explained in the next chapter. The social norms apply to all the children. They are dictated by the children in an unknown manner. It is still unclear how this happens and what the dynamic is that determines them, and more research is required in this area. Social norms require a very high level of commitment. Children don't wonder whether they are right or suitable for them. The moment they are established, they obey them in an internal, instinctive way, without any judgment. Children are not afraid of any authority. They act in order to be liked by others or to be good children in the eyes of others, as described in the developmental stages according to Colby and Kohlberg (1987, 2010). They obey the social norms on an instinctive level, as if they were the land upon which they had walked all their lives.

Socially rejected and unpopular children have difficulty in accepting the social norms. They check whether the norms suit them and usually feel that they don't. They often prefer the traditional rules of their teachers and parents, or their personal preferences, and reject the social norms. Some examples of rejecting the social norms and sticking to the parents' and teachers' morality: "The children in my class are rude to teachers and don't treat them well. I can't talk to teachers like that"; "I can't harm others"; "We have an autistic boy and they throw paper balls at him, I can't hurt a child like that"; "I like dressing a particular way. I buy my clothes where nobody else does. My clothes make me feel special, and I absolutely won't dress like all the other girls, who all wear the same things, ugly clothes". Social norms are arbitrary and can relate to any field: clothing and fashion, communication and speaking, culture and games.

Teachers and parents often resist the children's norms. Parents are often disturbed by the children's self-belittling and following the herd. Sometimes they object to norms that contradict their morality (such as buying expensive brands or a phone), oppose the shallow and arbitrary nature of the norms, and so, once again out of misunderstanding the developmental importance, they delay the developmental process. Often, when there's a clash between a social norm and a moral rule of the adults, the adults think that they can make the children obey then just as they did when the children were younger, in kindergarten and the first grade, but during the latency stage, this is no longer the case. Children stick to their norms, and *the adults have no influence over them*. At the same time, the parents and teachers have the impression that they can still reach the children's hearts and rekindle their morality. They are certain that they can make their children behave "nicely" again. In practice, the children behave "nicely", as the adults wish, only on the surface. Girls who are criticized for not including one of the class's girls and are educated by the homeroom teacher to treat that girl nicely and be her friend, nod and smile at the teacher and even fake an obedient expression. But when out of the teacher's sight, they will continue to treat that rejected girl in the same way, without changing their treatment of her at all.

Social norms also include issues related to the developmental topics mentioned earlier: separation between boys and girls, stereotypes, restraint, and delayed gratification. These developmental norms are just as binding as the arbitrary social norms. Children who refuse to observe these developmental norms, such as: boys who play with girls, boys who are good at chess when this doesn't suit the class norm of a certain computer game or soccer, boys who cry in classes where restraint is a norm – such children receive a strong sanction response just like breaking any arbitrary norm, like wearing a certain brand.

The society of children has a strong enforcement system. They don't let those who stray from the norms go. They sense any transgression, even the slightest, and immediately deal with it. At first, they take preliminary warning steps. The children approach those who disobey the norm and draw their attention to their not following the norm. If the children don't immediately change their behavior and accept the social norm, and continue behaving according to their own rules, further warnings are issued. When these steps fail to subordinate the children and they are consistent in rejecting social norms, then the social sanction is applied. One of my patients, who was severely rejected by the girls in her class, described repeated situations where a few girls followed her everywhere because she was known as a serial norm-breaker. They warned her repeatedly, but she continued to ignore them, and they started shouting at her loudly "You mustn't!" and made all the girls gather around her and start shouting at her.

Social rejection as a social sanction

Violating social norms leads to sanctions (Nichols, 2002). In situations where children don't accept the social norms, the society of children responds with a severe sanction: social rejection. Its familiar forms are: social rejection, ostracism, isolation, humiliation, verbal or physical violence, online bullying, and shaming. This deterring sanction damages the most significant need of this age – the need for social belonging. This sanction has a shocking and unsettling nature. Indeed, as we saw earlier, the implications of social rejection for children are serious and severe both in the present and in their impact on the children's future in all areas of functioning. Social rejection is a very powerful sanction with one goal: to enforce obedience. It is intended to deter, to threaten, and to force the children to adapt themselves to social norms and to subordinate themselves to the class hierarchy.

With all its cruelty, this social sanction has a supportive role in normative intrapsychic development. As with the Oedipal complex, where the fear of castration serves the developmental stage, so the fear of the social sanction serves the developmental stage of latency, since it contributes, through deterrence and threats, to the children's acceptance of the social hierarchy and norms. During latency, there is developmental importance to accepting and obeying arbitrary social norms, as will be discussed in the next chapter. The arbitrary rules must be obeyed even though they don't always contain logical content or internal moral meaning.

Examples of social sanctions:

- During the break, the fourth-grade girls were comparing their hair. They untied it and showed each other. When Kelly presented her curls, the girls started laughing and said, "You have sheep's wool!" From that day onward, whenever they saw her, they laughed at her and shouted: "Sheep's wool, sheep's wool!"
- The fifth-grade boys were getting ready for a soccer game in the afternoon, and only Sam wasn't invited to join them.
- The girls in class wrote curses on one girl's notebook and ostracized her.
- The boys threw one boy's bag into the schoolyard, scattering its contents and damaging the equipment and books.

Most of the teachers' interventions are intended to fight these social sanctions. Moral adults don't have the required tolerance of these serious behaviors, and rightly so. But once again, teachers and parents don't understand the developmental role the sanctions serve. Laughing at Kelly's curls informs her that in general she doesn't accept the social norms. Rejecting the social norms is apparent to the society of children whenever they are together, in each other's company. The rejection shown by their insulting attitude to her curls is the sanction. The society of girls is punishing her for not obeying the norms using a powerful, wide-ranging sanction that becomes relevant in every realm, place, and opportunity where they can apply it. Even the slightest violation of a social norm, such as preferring different music, playing a different game, trying to get appreciation from a teacher, or emphasizing personal uniqueness, leads to a very serious, wide-ranging sanction that doesn't allow the punished children one moment or one tiny space to breathe. The sanction is brutal, fully invading the entire psychic existence of the children who reject the social norms. The curly-haired girl who was given this severe sanction will henceforth be highly sensitive to social rejection. The experience of the upsetting social sanction will make her "straighten up" according to society's requirements, perhaps do whatever she can to straighten her hair, and be alert and sensitive to any way she differs from society. By sharpening her senses to perceiving social norms, she escapes any danger. From this moment onward, the girls won't comment on her hair any more, even if she doesn't end up straightening her curls.

The class norms and the sanctions shouldn't be confused. Writing curses on a rejected girl's notebook isn't the class norm. This is a sanction against her for her rejection of the social norms and hierarchy. The society of children is alert and sensitive to notice children who continue rejecting the norms despite warnings they have received. Often, such social sanctions serve as a wake-up call for children to adapt themselves to the behavior codes that are accepted by their age group. Children with sufficiently strong egos, despite experiencing negative feelings and emotions, will activate coping strategies of flexible adaptation and will return to the social center (Binstock, 2003). Experiencing a social sanction necessarily raises these children's awareness and caution regarding what is happening among their classmates. Increasing social alertness is an important and significant developmental move.

Social norms compared with sanctions

Sanctions are brutal in their disruptive force and are applied widely to the entire social existence (during classes, breaks, in the afternoon, during any activity). Social norms during latency, in contrast, are subtle and temporary. Social norms differ from universal moral norms, which have a deep internal significance. These are stable and permanent, constitute the foundation of the world, and are based on an indisputable higher authority. Class social norms during latency, conversely, are arbitrary and don't relate to deep moral values. They are shallow and external (all the girls wear a red scarf, all the children use a particular word, and so on). Latency age social norms can't be phrased or defined clearly and they can change from moment to moment. They pass by in the blink of an eye and take on various forms in the social realities of this age: playing, serving food, speech style, clothing, etc. They change quickly and the children acquire them rapidly (Schmidt, Rakoczy, & Tomasello, 2012). They can shift from game to game, from day to day, and even from moment to moment. Children with normal emotional development are flexible and capable of perceiving the changes in the norms and adapting themselves to them. The social norms during latency aren't fixed and can't be phrased in writing or even verbally. The purpose of latency age social norms is to support the development of the psychic subordination function, which will be explained later on.

Morality during latency

Strange as it may sound, the "cruel" phenomena listed at the beginning of the book are related to the most significant development during latency. Human beings are born with the ability to distinguish between good and bad, and to prefer the good. Studies show that babies have a preliminary sense of justice and an intuitive reaction to evil (Holvoet, Scola, Arciszewski, & Picard, 2016). It has also been found that children demonstrate love, sympathy, empathy, and pro-social behavior even prior to acquiring the family's moral norms (Turiel, 2006). These studies support the argument that morality doesn't develop internally and that it isn't learned or related to the parents' education. From birth, human beings possess the ability to judge morally without any influence of race, culture, and education (Mikhail, 2007). People's moral judgment capability is a survival advantage. This is an intuitive, sensory-affective, and automatic ability. The ability to judge morally stems from a strong internal feeling and is unrelated to logical arguments (Haidt, 2001). According to Freud, morality is fully established at the end of the Oedipal stage, when children internalize the family moral system, which becomes their superego, the conscience according to which they function morally throughout life (Freud, 1923). The family morality is usually related to the society-wide morality of the community in which the family lives. The central characteristic of this family morality is the fact that it's canonical, universal, and society-wide. It has as high a level of obligation as that granted to divine commandments. This is a permanent, absolute, and unchanging morality. Respect your mother and your father, put not a stumbling-block before the blind, and so on. Nucci, Turiel, and Encarnacion-Gawrych (1983) distinguish between family morality and social norms. Morality involves behavior that helps others and doesn't harm anyone. Social norms are arbitrary and culture-specific and relate to things like how to dress.

During latency, morality transitions from the family, canonical morality to the morality of social norms (Nucci, Turiel, & Encarnacion-Gawrych, 1983). Latency age children refer to social norms rather than to the family or school morality, and they don't listen to their innate moral intuition. From absolute, canonical, intuitive, and emotional family morality they start preferring the morality of arbitrary social norms, which often lack internal logic and which change according to the social winds (Rizzo et al., 2017; Mulvey et al., 2014). Often, the social norms completely contradict the canonical family morality. The big question that arises regarding the behavior of children during latency is how their moral development can be explained when they overwhelmingly and unambiguously operate only in accordance with the social norms that contradict the canonical family morality that was internalized recently, at the end of their Oedipal stage, and in contrast with their innate intuition? Why does this happen precisely during latency? What is the developmental role of this change during latency, and how does it expand and enrich people's moral ability during adulthood?

Piaget (1967) considered the development of moral thinking from two perspectives: awareness of justice and respect for the rules. Piaget studied the moral judgment of children and found that respecting the rules develops in four stages: sensory-motor, egocentric, cooperation, and social codes. The conscious awareness of justice develops in three stages: amorality, heteronomy, and independence. Piaget described a developmental process from external morality to internalized morality. The development starts in infancy, during the sensory-motor stage, where the condition is amorality. This is a stage of being unaware of the rules or of moral responsibility. At the age of 2–3 years, children develop a basic awareness of the rules, but only from an egocentric perspective, according to their personal criteria. This stage is heteronomous, where morality is external and determined by adults. Children believe that the rules were given by powerful authorities that demand obedience, and they obey the rules not because of any internal understanding of the purpose of the rules but due to the use of rewards and punishments aimed at helping them distinguish between right and wrong. At the age of 5–6 years, following the heteronomous stage, children understand that the rules enable society to function fairly and harmoniously. The process is completed around age 12, with the development of an independent morality, where they no longer depend on external factors to obey the laws but obey them independently. According to Piaget, the order of the stages is universal and unchanging, and each developmental stage contains the development of mental organization and structures that enable the transition to the next stage (Piaget, 1932).

Lawrence Kohlberg (1976) called his theory Cognitive Development, which occurs in a social and nonsocial context. Kohlberg based his theory on Piaget, who considered mature morality as logical and inherent to social relations. Colby and Kohlberg (2010) viewed morality as developing according to the developmental stages. They identified six groups of moral orientation, and divided them into three developmental levels:

1   Preconventional level: at the first level of morality, the moral intention is egocentric. Children act morally according to an orientation of rewards and punishments from authority figures.

2 Conventional level: the more developed level aimed at interpersonal partnership and being a good boy or girl in the eyes of others. Also, morality develops to an orientation of law and order as sacred.

3 Postconventional level: the highest moral level is the level of universal moral rules and also a personal conscience.

Most children aged 9 are at the second, conventional level (Li, 2016). The main axis of moral development, according to the cognitive approach, is the transition that occurs from the level of shallow and egocentric understanding and judgment, when children act morally due to obeying authority and considerations of rewards and punishments. At this stage of morality, it's difficult to compose an overall, cohesive picture of reality from several information sources and prominent stimuli are attractive in the here and now. In the more advanced developmental stage of morality, there is decentration (release from narrow and unbalanced attention), and morality is based on mutual norms, where there is an increase in centration and a rise in the mental integration ability and the need for balance, harmony, permanence, congruence, symmetry, and reducing cognitive dissonance (Gibbs, 2003). This development leads to morality that is profound and takes into consideration a range of factors.

What is relevant here is that according to Piaget and Kohlberg, morality that depends on authority, rewards, and punishments, or the desire to be a good boy or girl in others' eyes, is a morality that suits an earlier developmental stage than the stage where children obey social rules, as occurs during latency. In the eyes of adults, particularly teachers, children who obey the authority of teachers and behave in accordance with the canonical family moral values are perceived as good children, while children who operate according to the class norms, which often contradict moral values, and children who disobey the teachers' authority, are perceived as bad children or a bad class. In fact, according to the cognitive developmental theory, the opposite is true. The "bad" children are at a higher developmental stage than the "good" children.

I argue that the importance of moral development during latency – when children obey moral norms that are arbitrary, changing, relative, and not absolute; influenced by social factors such as social interests related to status and social power; and founded on mental considerations and strategies rather than on emotions and intuitions – is this: the social morality adds to the innate emotional-intuitive morality and the canonical family morality a new dimension of flexibility and variability. The intuitive, family, canonical morality is absolute and permanent and has a high level of commitment and loyalty. The mature morality includes the intuitive, emotional, permanent, and deterministic elements. Latency adds another component that expands the infinite freedom of choice. This component is the moral component whose foundation is social.

Empathy in latency

The theoretical definition of empathy is amorphic. It moves between an emotional process, a personality trait (hereditary), will-based, or a human strategy. The question at the basis of the study of empathy is whether empathy is emotional or cognitive – a structure composed of several processes, which is not fundamentally psychological, or a category of behaviors that are connected to each other on the basis of a psychological mechanism (Herrington, 2016). The professional literature distinguishes between emotional and cognitive empathy: cognitive empathy involves a precise perception of the other's emotions, cognitive perception of the other's viewpoint, or an emotional theory of mind (Walter, 2012). Emotional empathy, in contrast, is defined as less perceptive and more emotional and involving the experience of emotions in response to the other's emotions.

During elementary school, common social phenomena clearly lack morality and empathy at the levels that were achieved at earlier stages of development: bullying and victimization, violence, humiliation, ostracism, shaming, and so on. Children who are developed in both morality and empathy, who at the age of 5 showed sympathy and compassion for others' suffering, during latency start behaving without empathy toward their classmates who are in insufferable distress. Various studies have shown confusing findings regarding the level of empathy during middle childhood, particularly in the context of bullying and victimization. According to Martin Hoffman (2000), empathy develops throughout life, starting with preliminary empathy that starts during infancy using primitive mechanisms such as: imitation, conditioning, and association, up to mature empathy, in which there is social cognitive development, relying on the development of the self as distinct from others. A number of studies also indicate an increase in the empathy level. However, other studies show that there is a decline in empathy during latency. A review by Van Noorden and others (2014) found that while some studies reported negative correlations between empathy and bullying, as would be expected, other studies didn't find such a connection and even reported a positive correlation between the two variables, meaning an increase in the level of bullying correlated with an increase in cognitive empathy (Williford et al., 2016).

From my clinical experience, latency age patients often speak about the expression of empathy as something "fake" or "hypocritical". They interpret expressions of empathy toward socially popular people as follows: "The girls only pretend to understand the class queen. When she cries, they all run to her and comfort her. But it's hypocritical and fake. They don't really care". In contrast, there's almost never any expression of empathy toward socially rejected or unpopular children. The thing that most surprised me as a therapist: children who were socially rejected and improved their social status reacted, after improving their situation, toward other children in the class who became socially rejected and occupied their previous place with a complete lack of empathy and were unable to relate to their suffering in any way. As much as I tried to remind them how they had suffered, this didn't change their inability to feel the suffering of the rejected children at all. The emotional, instinctive empathy that younger children feel toward the suffering of others doesn't exist during latency. Like morality, the empathy that exists at this age is intellectual, manipulative, and operates solely in the service of social interests. The children are busy acquiring social status and act, through the use of strategies including "group social empathy", to achieve this purpose. They don't do this through deep and empathic interpersonal relationships. For instance, the class queen usually behaves without empathy toward the unpopular girls, and they take this for granted. "When the class queen wants something, everyone gives it to her. She doesn't care if this is an expensive item or game". Even the girl whose item or game was taken isn't upset. She accepts the reality that determines that the class queen has privileges. "You have to give the class king what he wants because he's the king! You give only to him. He doesn't give me anything, only I have to give him!"

In contrast, the socially rejected children have great difficulty with this. They still feel the intuitive empathy and feel there is injustice in cases where emotional empathy is lacking. One of the patients who was instructed to behave like the other children and give up what was his in favor of the class king described his feeling:

> I understand that I have to give him what he wants, even though in my heart I think he doesn't deserve it. He also destroys everything he takes, and why should I agree that he should destroy my game? Apart from this, he never gives me anything.

The rejected children find it hard to accept that the class rulers treat them and everyone else arbitrarily, without empathy, and unjustly. The lack of instinctive emotional empathy is expressed, perhaps at the highest level, in the responses of the socially rejected children: "I ask them to join in a soccer game, and they say: 'No! You're bad!'"; "When I reach the bench, everyone pushes me and runs away from me"; "If I get close to three girls who are talking, they tell me: 'Go away, this is a private conversation!'". In my experience, my efforts to increase empathy toward children in the class failed. When I tried, for example, to present to my patient the difficulty of one of the popular children he hated, who had lost his mother and was emotionally neglected by his father, he responded: "So what if he doesn't have a mother and his dad isn't at home. His uncle is rich and buys him presents. He's not unfortunate".

References

Ashton, P.T. (2006). Middle childhood: Period of latency or context of development? [Review of the book *Developmental Contexts in Middle Childhood: Bridges to Adolescence and Adulthood*, edited by A.C. Huston & M.N. Ripke]. *PsycCRITIQUES*, 51(39).

Bartsch, K. & Wellman, H.M. (1995). *Children Talk about the Mind*. New York, NY, US: Oxford University Press.

Becker, T.E. (1974). On latency. *Psychoanalytic Study of the Child*, 29: 3–11.

Binstock, O. (2003). *The Phenomenological Aspect of Social Rejection by Peers among Socially Normal Students in Elementary and Junior High School*. Ph.D. Dissertation. Jerusalem: Hebrew University [Hebrew].

Colby, A. & Kohlberg, L. (2010). *The Measurement of Moral Judgment* (Vol. 1). Cambridge, UK: Cambridge University Press. (First published in 1987).

Erikson, E.H. (1950). *Childhood and Society*. New York: Norton.

Freud, A. (1936). *The Ego and the Mechanisms of Defence*. London: Hogarth Press and Institute of Psycho-Analysis. (Revised edition: 1966 (US), 1968 (UK)).

Freud, S. (1914). On narcissism. *The Standard Edition of the Complete Psychological Works of Sigmund Freud*, 14: 67–102.

Freud, S. (1923/1949). *The Ego and the Id*. Trans. J. Riviere. London: Hogarth Press.

Gibbs, J.C. (2003). *Moral Development and Reality: Beyond the Theories of Kohlberg*. Thousand Oaks, CA: Hoffman, Sage Publication.

Greene, M.L., Griggs, M.S., Mikami, A.Y., & Rimm-Kaufman, S.E. (2016). Classroom quality and student behavior trajectories in elementary school. *Psychology in the Schools*, 53(7): 690–704.

Haidt, J. (2001). The emotional dog and its rational tail: A social intuitionist approach to moral judgment. *Psychological Review*, 108: 814–834.

Harris, J.R. (1998). *The Nurture Assumption: Why Children Turn Out the Way They Do*. New York: Free Press.

Harter, S. & Buddin, B.J. (1987). Children's understanding of the simultaneity of two emotions: A five-stage developmental acquisition sequence. *Developmental Psychology*, 23(3): 388–399.

Herrington, J.D. (2016). Commentary: Cognitive and emotional empathy in transdiagnostic research: Reflections on Klapwijk et al. *Journal of Child Psychology and Psychiatry*, 57(6): 748–749.

Hoffman, M.L. (2000). *Empathy and Moral Development: Implications for Caring and Justice*. New York: Cambridge University Press.

Hofmann, S.G. & Doan, S.N. (2018). *The Social Foundations of Emotion: Developmental, Cultural, and Clinical Dimensions*. Washington, DC: American Psychological Association.

Holvoet, C., Scola, C., Arciszewski, T., & Picard, D. (2016). Infants' preference for prosocial behaviors: A literature review. *Infant Behavior & Development*, 45(Part B): 125–139.

Hughes, D., Del, T.J., Harding, J., Way, N., & Rarick, J. (2016). Trajectories of discrimination across adolescence: Associations with academic, psychological and behavioral outcomes. *Child Development*, 87: 1337–1351.

Kaplan, E.B. (1965). Reflections regarding psychomotor activities during the latency period. *Psychoanalytic Study of the Child*, 20: 220–238.

Kohlberg, L. (1976). Moral stages and moralization: The cognitive-developmental approach. In *Moral Development and Behavior: Theory, Research, and Social Issues*, edited by T. Lickona (pp. 31–53). Holt, NY: Rinehart and Winston.

Kohut, H. (1971). *The Analysis of the Self*. New York: International Universities Press.

Li, S. (2016). A mechanism for gratitude development in a child. *Early Child Development and Care*, 186(3): 466–479.

Mahler, M.S. (1975). On the current status of the infantile neurosis. *Journal of the American Psychoanalytic Association*, 23(2): 327–333.

Malatesta, C.Z., Culver, C., Tesman, J.R., & Shepard, B. (1989). The development of emotion expression during the first two years of life. *Monographs of the Society for Research in Child Development*, 54(1–2): 1–104.

Mikhail, J. (2007). Universal moral grammar: Theory, evidence and the future. *Trends in Cognitive Science*, 11: 143–152.

Mulvey, K.L., Hitti, A., Rutland, A., Abrams, D., & Killen, M. (2014). Context differences in children's ingroup preferences. *Developmental Psychology*, 50(5): 1507–1519.

Nantel-Vivier, A., Kokko, K., Caprara, G.V., Pastorelli, C., Gerbino, M.G., Paciello, M., Côté, S., Pihl, R.O., Vitaro, F., & Tremblay, R. (2009). Prosocial development from childhood to adolescence: A multi-informant perspective with Canadian and Italian longitudinal studies. *Journal of Child Psychology and Psychiatry*, 50(5): 590–598.

Nichols, T.R. (2002). Adolescent social competence: An examination of social skills, social performance, and social adjustment with urban minority youth. *Dissertation Abstracts International, Section B: The Sciences and Engineering*, 63(3-B): 1589.

Nucci, L., Turiel, E., & Encarnacion-Gawrych, G. (1983). Children's social interactions and social concepts: Analyses of morality and convention in the Virgin Islands. *Journal of Cross-Cultural Psychology*, 14(4): 469–487.

Over, H., Carpenter, M. (2013). The social side of imitation. *Child Development Perspectives*, 7(1): 6–11.

Piaget, J. (1932). *The Moral Development of the Child*. London: Kegan Paul.

Piaget, J. (1967). *Six Psychological Studies*. New York: Random House.

Rapaport, D. (1967). *The Collected Papers of David Rapaport*, edited by M.M. Gill. New York: Basic Books.

Rizzo, M.T., Cooley, S., Elenbaas, L., & Killen, M. (2017). Young children's inclusion decisions in moral and social: Conventional group norm context. *Journal of Experimental Child Psychology*, 165: 19–36.

Rodkin, P.C., Ryan, A.M., Jamison, R., & Wilson, T. (2012). Social goals, social behavior, social status in middle childhood. *Developmental Psychology*, 49(6): 1139–1150.

Rutland, A. & Killen, M. (2015). A developmental science approach to reducing prejudice and social exclusion: Intergroup processes, social-cognitive development and moral reasoning. *Social Issues and Policy Review*, 9: 121–154.

Rutland, A. & Killen, M. (2017). Fair resource allocation among children and adolescents: The role of group and developmental processes. *Child Development Perspectives*, 11(1): 56–62.

Sarnoff, C.A. (1976). *Latency*. Northvale, NJ: Aronson.

Schilbach, L., Eickhoff, S.B., Rotarska-Jagiela, A., Fink, G.R., & Vogeley, K. (2008). Minds at rest? Social cognition as the default mode of cognizing and its putative relationship to the "default system" of the brain. *Consciousness and Cognition: An International Journal*, 17(2): 457–467.

Schmidt, M.F.H., Rakoczy, H., & Tomasello, M. (2012). Young children enforce social norms selectively depending on the violator's group affiliation. *Cognition*, 124(3): 325–333.

Selman, R.L. & Byrne, D.F. (1974). A structural-developmental analysis of levels of role taking in middle childhood. *Child Development*, 45: 803–806.

Shustorovich, E. & Weinstein, L. (2010). Universal fantasy in latency: Separation, attachment sexuality in Julio Cortázar's "Bestiary". *The International Journal of Psychoanalysis*, 91(6): 1465–1482.

Sroufe, L.A., Cooper, R.G., & DeHart, G.B. (1996). *Child Development: Its Nature and Course* (3rd ed.). Boston: McGraw Hill.

Sullivan, H.S. (1933). *Personal Psychopathology: Early Formulations*. New York: Norton, 1972.

Sullivan, H.S. (1953). *The Interpersonal Theory of Psychiatry*. New York: Norton.

Turiel, E. (2006). The development of morality. In *Handbook of Child Psychology, Social, Emotional, and Personality Development*, edited by N. Eisenberg (pp. 789–857). Hoboken, NJ: Wiley.

Van Noorden, T.H., Haselager, G.J., Cillessen, A.H., & Bukowski, W.M. (2014). Empathy and involvement in bullying in children and adolescents: A systematic review. *Journal of Youth and Adolescence*, 44: 637–657.

Walter, H. (2012). Social cognitive neuroscience of empathy: Concepts, circuits, and genes. *Emotion Review*, 4: 9–17.

Williford, A., Boulton, A., Forrest, B.S.S., Bender, K.A., Dieterich, W.A., & Jenson, J.M. (2016). The effect of bullying and victimization on cognitive empathy development during the transition to middle school. *Child & Youth Care Forum*, 45(4): 525–541.

Winnicott, D.W. (1951/1958). Transitional objects and transitional phenomena. In *Collected Papers: Through Paediatrics to Psycho-Analysis*. London: Tavistock.

Zimmer-Gembeck, M.J., Nesdale, D., Webb, H.J., Khatibi, M., & Downey, G. (2016). A longitudinal rejection sensitivity model of depression and aggression: Unique roles of anxiety, anger, blame, withdrawal, and retribution. *Journal of Abnormal Child Psychology*, 44(7): 1291.

3 Analogy

The self as a biological cell

First, let's present a review of the characteristics and qualities of latency that were presented in the previous chapter and their place within a psychoanalytic paradigm that explains the development occurring during latency. A recent article by Rutland and Killen (2017) describes the development during latency as follows:

> From approximately 7 to 8 years, children develop a theory of social mind. They begin to appreciate that the emotions and intentions they attribute to individuals or groups within social relationships are not always the same as those held by the self. These social-cognitive developments contribute to a more advanced understanding of groups and how they function, and the ability from middle childhood to differentiate one's own viewpoint from that held by groups when deciding how to allocate resources. From this developmental point, as children become adolescents, they begin to reflect on many group norms at different levels when deciding how to allocate resources. In a recent study, those in middle childhood (as opposed to adolescence) were influenced by their own group's competitive norms and paid little attention to a generic norm when allocating resources.
>
> (Rutland & Killen, 2017: 57)

Also, articles from the past 25 years of brain research indicate the existence of a social part, including brain areas such as the superior temporal sulcus, the temporo-parietal junction, the temporal poles, the medial prefrontal cortex, the anterior cingulate cortex, the amygdala, and the insula (Adolphs, 2003; Frith, 2007).

My argument is that the latency stage is more than cognitive development as described in this citation. This is whole psyche development. The development of the social part is not just a theory that develops in the children's minds. During latency, the psyche operates in the new part that awakens at this age. I call this part of the self: the social self. This is the part that was dormant and inactive during early childhood (up to age 5 to 7, the end of the Oedipal stage), and it awakens in the same way that erogenous organs awaken during the early development stages. But this part isn't a physical erogenous organ, but a part whose addition to the self enables spiritual existence in the human psyche. Children at a particular stage are focused, enthusiastic, excited, interested, flourishing, and enjoying everything related to the organ of that developmental stage (for example, the mouth during the oral stage), and their enthusiasm fades when they transition into the next stage where their enthusiasm is transferred to another erogenous organ. The same is true for children during latency. When the social self part awakens, the early erogenous organs fade and no longer stimulate them as in the previous stages. They focus on the social experience that is essentially different from their infantile physical experience. This is a new experience that causes them excitement and enthusiasm; it entirely encompasses them. This is an experience that *is* the child himself or herself. The self during latency is in the social experience, and this is the experience where the self lives and focuses.

Now let's list all the changes that occur during latency, as described above, and then place them in a formula.

The changes that occur during latency

- Transition from sexuality to asexuality.
- Transition from boy-girl love during kindergarten to repulsion and separation between the sexes, a process that occurs between third and fifth grade.
- Transition from the parents as selfobjects, as significant figures who nurture and fulfill needs, to a society of classmates that fulfills needs.
- Transition from the dominance of the authority of parents, kindergarten teachers, and first-grade teachers to the authority of the society of classmates.
- Transition from the family rules of morality, which are part of the general society's morality, to the social norms of the children's specific class.
- Transition from being nourished to providing nourishing to the class king or class queen.
- Transition from individual drives and desires as establishing and creating change in reality to accepting the drives and desires of others as establishing and creating change in reality.
- Transition from fulfilling the children's grandiose need for admiration – "the most special, the best in the world" – to grandiose satisfaction from the society of classmates' praise for being "the most prominent in being similar to everyone else".

- Transition from controlling the parents, where the children "rule" their parents who adapt themselves to the children's needs, and even defer their own needs to fulfill their children's needs, to a situation where the "class rulers" control the class and rule the children.
- Transition from a feeling of "I'm omnipotent" to a situation where the society of classmates is "omnipotent".
- Transition from friendship with an interpersonal best friend to friendship groups based on the hierarchy (from loyal best friends to popular friends).
- Transition from instinctive emotional empathy to social-intellectual, manipulative empathy that serves social needs.
- Transition from direct, honest, and real expression of personal desires to social expression that isn't honest and often even requires lying and hiding personal intentions and desires.
- Transition from difficulty in regulation and delaying gratification to the ability to show restraint.
- Transition from expressing emotions directly and clearly using physical sensory means, such as crying, stamping, or head shaking, to indicate refusal to verbal expression that doesn't necessarily match the inner emotion.

When we place all these characteristics into a formula we obtain the following understanding: The latency age indicates a transition from a quality that is emotional-sensory, egocentric, grandiose, omnipotent, built of interpersonal relationships – the stage where the parents are the significant figures in children's lives, with the individual standing in the center showing "willfulness", uncompromising, and the world showing flexibility and satisfying every need – to a quality where individuals must adapt themselves to others, to the group hierarchy, in which others rule and control. Personal drives and desires are reined in and hidden. Behavior and speech are based only on social interests rather than personal desires. Children learn to bend through a flexible psychic ability of becoming "subordinate" to someone else's center, to social rules that aren't the self's own rules.

During latency, the psychic function of "subordination" is established. At the end of latency, from adolescence onward, people move between these two psychic functions: the first is infantile-interpersonal, with an uncompromising nature, and its morality is absolute, unchanging, totally binding, and deterministic. The second function is social, and its character changes. Its morality is relative, not binding, and is compromising, varying according to social circumstances. These are two important functions, and both are equally important. We can achieve nothing in life without using these two functions. In order to achieve any goal, large or small, a personal goal, a personal desire, we must adapt ourselves to our surroundings. We must have very sharp senses to perceive and understand our environment, to perceive what's important in society, what the hierarchy is, who decides, and what's allowed and forbidden in society. People can't operate according to their desires alone; they must act within a society by constantly adapting themselves to its rules. Also, people can't operate according to fixed and dominant internal principles and rules in a way that doesn't enable flexibility and consideration of the various, changing social situations and norms.

Latency and the "subordination" function lead people to a higher level of morality, in which there are no fixed commandments or uncompromising procedural rules that don't take the circumstances into account and follow the maximal spirit of the law. Behaving exclusively according to absolute-canonical morality doesn't enable freedom of choice. The morality of latency adds complexity to the freedom of choice. It's relative, mutable, and not instinctive but employs judgment, social interests, and considerations, which sometimes contradict the natural instinct of basic morality that exists within people to allow them to distinguish between good and evil. During latency, this function awakens and social matters, including social rejection, serve individuals in developing the flexibility required by this function. In addition, this stage sharpens children's sensitivity to perceive the subtleties of social norms, which are by their very nature arbitrary, rapidly changing, but critical for fitting in and achieving goals. People have to adapt themselves to the rules of their school or job in order to advance themselves, their ambitions, and their goals. They reach higher achievements when society doesn't oppose them. When they are more flexible in adapting themselves to society, they will also be appreciated and promoted.

This dynamic between "willfulness" and "subordination" also develops throughout life. It reaches a peak when the personal desires merge with social desires, so that individuals find themselves working within society, on behalf of themselves and of society, for the benefit of themselves and of society, when all these things blend into one. To conclude, during latency there is a transition from the infantile part of the early years of development to a new part that awakens during latency. The transition is from the part of the childhood self, whose essence is a condition of "willfulness" (egocentric, grandiose, and so on) to the social self part, whose condition is "subordination".

Developmental paradigm: the existence of the self in analogy to a biological cell

Brain research studies indicate the development of the social brain throughout all the various developmental stages (Braams & Crone, 2017). I wish to argue that the development of the social brain should be viewed in a wider context of the development of the self. I argue that the self's developmental paradigm can be sketched in analogy to a biological cell.

From birth until the age of 5 to 7, children undergo familiar developmental stages, based on established theories such as those of: Freud, Klein, Mahler, Winnicott, Erikson, and others.

Around the ages of 5 to 7, the Oedipal stage ends, and around 6 to 8 years a new stage begins: latency. This stage ends at adolescence. During latency, all the early developmental stages are blocked. This blocking consolidates all the early stages into one part, an area I call the childhood self. From the age of 7 to 8, the self moves into existing in a new part, the social self.

> **Childhood self:** from birth until the age of 5 to 7, including all the developmental stages that occur during these ages. This part is consolidated and blocked during latency. The childhood self always exists in the function of "willfulness".
>
> **Social self:** awakens during latency and is in essence the function of "subordination".
>
> **Self core membrane:** during latency, blocks the part of the childhood self. Its entire role during latency is to seal off the contents of the childhood self and turn it into the self core. During adolescence and later in life, the membrane serves to transfer contents, interpret, mediate, and translate between the two parts, the childhood self and the social self. These two parts of the self are so different in their being and essence that they almost cannot exist in one entity. This is what makes the membrane's mediating and translating function so important. In latency, it doesn't yet fulfill this role. At this age, the membrane's sole function is to block the childhood self part (self core), which doesn't allow latency age children to be in contact with this part. In latency, children exist in the social self part without any contact with the childhood self part. The membrane doesn't function until adolescence.
>
> **How the self functions from adolescence onward:** from adolescence onward, all the parts of the self function at full capacity. The childhood self functions like the "cell's core". The social self functions like the "cytoplasm". The "self core membrane" functions like the "cell membrane", located between the two other parts.

Blocking the childhood self

During latency, the childhood self part is blocked and consolidated into the self core. Similar to the contact barrier (Bion, 1977), which normally prevents components belonging to a different state of consciousness from disturbing the current state, the "membrane" is what blocks it. The self during latency exists only in the social self part (the social self cytoplasm). At this stage, the membrane doesn't yet function as a translator or mediator between the two parts. The membrane begins to function only at the end of latency and start of adolescence.

This clear distinction, that during latency the self only exists in the social self part in the function of "subordination", became clear to me during therapy. Let me present one case study to demonstrate this issue. All the patients who came to me suffering from social rejection due to immature behaviors in the willfulness function: playing with members of the opposite sex; a need for interpersonal friendship and unwillingness to accept the change to group friendship; dependence on adult selfobjects such as parents and teachers; obeying parents and teachers; sticking to the family morality while rejecting class norms; wanting to be rewarded and recognized for being a "good child"; rejecting behaviors that violate teachers' authority; not accepting the authority of class rulers; fighting to satisfy personal wishes and rejecting the group's will; the need for solo admiration and unwillingness to be like everyone else; difficulty in delaying satisfaction; and childish reactions such as crying and physical violence.

The understanding that the self in latency migrates into existing in the social self part was strengthened by the evidence of the cases I treated. Existence in the social self part is exclusive, with no existence in the self core. This part is blocked and inaccessible. I shall present this understanding using Andy's case study.

Andy's case study

Andy's parents took him to therapy due to his difficulty in interpreting social situations. It's worth mentioning that most children who encounter social difficulties are referred to therapy with the diagnosis "difficulty in interpreting social situations" or "difficulty in reading the social map". During my first session with them, the parents said that Andy said he was lonely, he had no friends, and that the boys insulted and offended him and refused to include him in their games and activities. He often responded by bursting into tears and becoming violent: biting and hitting them. The teacher also reported to the parents that Andy was lonely during breaks and often wanted to demonstrate his superiority over others, which led to their aversion to him.

During my first session with Andy, he described situations where he was unwilling to participate in a regular game with the boys, where they punch each other. He described a situation where the boys were wrestling in a group and punching each other. The group approached him, and one boy turned to Andy and told him to punch him on the shoulder. Andy felt pressured by this demand directed at him. He experienced a serious conflict. On the one hand, his parents had educated him to nonviolence, and he was a peace-loving child, but on the other hand the boys were requiring him to punch another boy hard, something he was unable to do. As a compromise, he gave a weak punch, which led to a severe reaction of ridicule and rejection: "Sissy! Gay!", and in response Andy burst into tears and started hitting and pushing the boys wildly. He also spoke to his homeroom teacher and told her about the boys' behavior, asking her to punish them.

During this session, Andy also described other situations. He was playing soccer, stole the ball from the "class king" and scored a goal, and instead of the boys appreciating this, thanking him, and cheering him, the "class king" attacked him and shouted at him, and all the boys started attacking him. He described situations where the boys ridiculed him for playing with a girl, his friend. The boys also often insulted him by saying he was as chatty as the girls.

An analysis of the first session raised the picture that Andy was still in the childhood function of "willfulness". He was subject to the parents' morality (nonviolence), and he expressed his frustration and pain in a way appropriate to the earlier developmental stage, by crying and using physical violence. He preferred to play with girls and also preferred an interpersonal type of friendship. He still expected to receive the grandiose attention of being in the center, being the best (scoring a goal), and was unwilling to subordinate himself and to allow the "class king" to score the goal for the team. He tended to chat, with the girls and in general, which did not fit the stereotype of boys at this age.

During the session, Andy said: "If you try to do both, it's worse than just going along with what I want. Because it's like mixing vinegar with drinking soda powder, like Coca Cola and Mentos. It creates an explosion. If I do both, give a punch but a weak one, the boys are most cruel towards me. If I'd told them: 'No! I don't hit', they would have been less cruel. And if I'd punched hard, I would have belonged among them and they would have appreciated me". Indeed, a weak punch, constituting a compromise between the social norm (a strong punch on the shoulder) and the parents' morality (not harming others), is impossible and awakens an immediate response of social rejection.

Latency contains only one possibility: behaving like everyone else. It is completely impossible for children to exist in the grandiose condition and also to be "subordinate" and accept the "rule of the class ruler", except for the class king and class queen, of course. It is impossible to be both at the center and accepted in the group. It is impossible to behave in a childish way (crying, violent outbursts, appealing to the teacher) and to be popular. All of these childhood experiences are blocked by the "membrane", and therefore during latency there is no connection to the childhood part of "willfulness". There is only one existence, that of subordination in the social self.

The self as a biological cell

Several developmental theories exist regarding the development of the self. Rochat (2009) argues that there are six possibilities ranging from self-obliviousness to self-consciousness. Neisser (1988) focused on five types of self-knowledge that build various aspects of the self (ecological, conceptual, private, extended, and interpersonal). Hofmann and Doan (2018) constructed a model whereby the self develops throughout childhood, and the self core is gradually gathered into the social self. They propose that babies have a preliminary sense of self from birth. They call this primal sensation the "self core". The self core distinguishes between the self and the physical surroundings. It does this unconsciously. The social world is the entire world. The self core develops over time and forms a social self that grows and becomes what distinguishes between the self and the social surroundings. In adulthood, the social world merges with the self and they call this self the "social self". The social self includes the self core. Thus, the feelings we experience pass through the filter of the social self.

I would like to propose a different perspective on the development of the self. According to this perspective, the self develops in analogy to the biological cell. In this, I am following the scientific trend in psychology, which derives models from other bodily systems such as excretion and breathing, and from physics and chemistry. Models are concrete analogies to the relationship we are attempting to describe. The image is vivid and thus easily understandable (Symington & Symington, 1996). The understanding arising from latency shows that the self core develops during the early years of development up to latency, and from latency the self starts to exist in a new part of the self, without contact with the self core. From adolescence, the self can be seen as analogous to the biological cell, including: the self core, the social self, and a third area, the membrane, which mediates between these two parts of the self.

A biological cell is the basic unit of life that contains all the features of life. All living organisms are composed of cells. The cell is composed of various parts, between which complex, multi-system dynamics exist. The purposes of the cell's existence: nourishing the individual cell, nourishing the entire group of cells in the living organism, and fulfilling a specific role within the system in which it exists. In analogy to the individual cell, we can view the self as a basic human unit that contains all the features of being human. When human society is composed of many "selves", the purposes of the self are to be nourished in its own existence, to nourish others, and to play a role in the social system in which it exists. We can use the basic intra-cellular dynamic to understand the intrapsychic dynamic on the basic level.

In the most general outline, we can describe the biological cell as follows:

The biological cell's core contains the vast majority of the hereditary material existing in the cell. The core's roles include, among other things, maintaining the genes it contains and controlling the expression of these genes in each cell.

The core membrane is a sort of envelope around the cell, which has two layers. Its role is to separate the core and its contents from the cytoplasm. The core membrane is impenetrable to most molecules. There is a system of pores spread around the membrane that enables certain molecules to move into the core and out of the core into the cytoplasm. The cell's core doesn't contain any membranes dividing it into sub-cores. Its contents are not uniform, and there are several intra-core bodies and structures. The best-known structure is the nucleolus, composing the ribosomes, which are responsible for translating the contents of the cell's core outwards.

The self core, according to this analogy, includes, in addition to psychological and cultural genetic baggage (Jung), also a range of psychic qualities familiar from the psychoanalytical theories regarding the first five to six years of life.

The psychic materials in the self core subconsciously influence people and exist in a form similar to "particles" in quantum physics, meaning that they have a material, finite, and deterministic existence.

The membrane separates within the self between the inner-psychic function, the childhood self, and the external psychic function, the social self. The self core membrane is a sort of intermediate "consciousness adjacent" space through which, like the core membrane in the biological cell, psychic materials move back and forth, inward and outward, as sort of messengers of the subconscious and the conscious, of the inner-psychic reality and the external psychic reality within the self. During latency, the membrane is not yet fully operational in the transition between the two parts: the infantile and the social. Its role during latency is purely blocking; to block the childhood self part. The self core membrane defines and limits the self core, seals it up with all its contents, the structures that developed up to the end of the Oedipal stage, and turns it into the person's innermost, most private place – the self core. This is a place that is difficult for our consciousness to access.

During latency, with the blocking of the childhood self in the self core, the contents of the childhood self become unconscious. Sealing the self core membrane makes the contents of the childhood self into basic materials that join the genetic psychic materials, and together they constitute the self core's elements. These are the elements that unconsciously dictate to people their existence in the world in their own unique, individual way and quality.

One of the familiar phenomena that support this developmental process is "childhood amnesia". This is how Freud describes it:

> The particular amnesia which, in the case of most people, though by no means all, hides the earliest beginnings of their childhood up to their sixth or eighth year. Hitherto it has not occurred to us to feel any astonishment at the fact of this amnesia, though we might have had good grounds for doing so. For we learn from other people that during these years, of which at a later date we retain nothing in our memory but a few unintelligible and fragmentary recollections, we reacted in a lively manner to impressions, that we were capable of expressing pain and joy in a human fashion, that we gave evidence of love, jealousy and other passionate feelings. [. . .] And of all this we, when we are grown up, have no knowledge of our own! Why should our memory lag so far behind the other activities of our minds? We have, on the contrary, good reason to believe that there is no period at which the capacity for receiving and reproducing impressions is greater than precisely during the years of childhood.
>
> (Freud, 1905: 174–175)

From the end of latency, at the start of adolescence and throughout life after that, the membrane is fully functional and transfers from and into the self core new information and emotional content from the social self, very selectively, and also transmits from the self core through the social self to the external surroundings nourishing materials or requests for nourishment. The great importance of this understanding is that all the childhood contents, up to the end of the genital-Oedipal stage, become sealed by the self core membrane (defense mechanisms), which turns them into basic materials that join the genetic psychic materials and constitute the foundation of the self core. These are the foundations that unconsciously dictate to people their unique existence in the world with their specific qualities that are theirs alone. The self core membrane starts operating during latency, employing only the blocking function, and is strengthened by a familiar but mysterious and undeciphered phenomenon of latency, the "childhood amnesia", described by Freud.

According to Freud, during latency the barriers rise organically. These barriers, using the analogy of the self as a cell, serve as the "self core membrane", block the early emotional contents and seal them within the self core, so they aren't accessible to memory and consciousness. We can also attribute to the role of the self core membrane Anna Freud's observation that during latency there is a development in the defense mechanisms so that all the ego's defense mechanisms are available to children and help them acquire greater control of the surroundings and develop a sense of reality versus the pleasure principle (Freud, A., 1936).

Another role of the self core membrane is regulating the drives of the self core. Support for this can be found in the work of Anna Ornstein, who noted three features of latency:

1 A rise in the consolidation of the self core, particularly the sense of control and competence.
2 Consolidation of the system of regulating self-value.
3 Progress in moral development.

(Ornstein, 1986: 15)

Applying the insights of Anna Ornstein to the analogy of the self as a cell, we can consider the role of the self core membrane as sealing the self core, leading to an increase in the sense of consolidation, control, and competence. Also, the blocking of the early childhood drives and contents by the self core membrane strengthens the regulation system, and the transition to the social self enhances the individual's adaptation to society's system of moral rules.

During latency, the social part awakens and the self core is blocked by the membrane. During latency, the membrane has no role except blocking the self core, and the self transitions to existing solely in the social part.

The Social Self Cytoplasm (SSC): the external part of the self, the social part, the experience of "us". "Our right-centric brain attends to 'we'" and experiences "the world of relationships as it is emerging in the moment" (Badenoch, 2016: 2), the state of the selfobject, the part that comes into contact with the external-social reality. It's the style, the culture, the conscious part. Brain science research has found that the part of the brain called the insula contains the social emotions and conscious processes (Hofmann & Doan, 2018). It's the existence of the idealizatory axis, the state of the self as participating in the world in a way that transcends itself and acting for the benefit of others, altruism. Like the state of a "wave" in quantum physics, it's infinite. This is the part that restores to psychoanalysis a philosophical position of idealism, which positions the human spirit as the factor that constitutes its world. The motivating psychic force here isn't a drive, but the attractive force of the highest purpose (Kolke, 2010). But the psyche of latency age children isn't there yet. It doesn't function fully. It exists in the part of the social self. The transition from an inner-psychic reality to the social self and the external-social reality occurs through a familiar phenomenon of latency. Group twinship is achieved through strict adherence to social norms, maintained by the threat of social rejection. The severe and arbitrary social norms, determined by the society of children and obediently observed, and also the serious pressure and threat of social rejection of children who disobey them, constitute a powerful social force for children. This helps their intrapsychic development by accelerating the delayed development processes of consolidating and reducing the materials of the self core, particularly by regulating drives and completing developmental processes including: separation from early objects and reducing grandiosity, omnipotence, exhibitionism, and exclusive control. The psychic quality required for accepting and obeying the social norms is "subordination", meaning the ability to concede, relinquishing and subordinating individual desires and principles. In addition, during the second stage of the latency period, the subordination ability is a function of mediation and compromise.

"Group twinship" and shared social norms are crucially important for continued development. When the group members have a system of norms and all the individuals follow it and live according to its orders, this enables mutuality in providing nurturing for the group's individual members (similar to Durkheim's view in his work *The Elementary Forms of Religious Life*). This means that people naturally feel the need to protect and help others in their group. Individuals who don't accept the shared norms won't receive the nurturing of "twinship".

The general scheme of the dynamics between the areas of the self: the self, like the biological cell, exists within a tissue of living cells in the social fabric of mutual nurturing, cooperation, coordination, organization, shared goals, and so on. The individual self, like the biological cell, is simultaneously nourished and nourishing. External and internal materials pass through the self core membrane, inward to the self core and outward to the social self, and from there out to the entire social human reality. Internal materials that come out of the self core seek a nourishing response in the social self from the external environment. When the response of the environment, society, and the selfobject is insufficient, the materials of the self core are sent back inward and outward to obtain a response that will enable the self's continued healthy existence within the social fabric in which it resides. Up to the end of the Oedipal stage, the self is still in the position of "receiving nourishment". From latency onward, the self has an additional part of "providing nourishment". This part develops during adolescence into the spiritual part that continues to grow and develop throughout life. The transition between the two parts of the self, the two contents of the self (which are essentially different), isn't enabled in a natural, direct path, but requires translation and coding that occurs in the self core membrane. The transition between the two states – from "willfulness" in the self core, a state of being nourished, grandiose, egocentric, and omnipotent, willfully in the center of the world that focuses only on me, to a state of "subordination" in the SSC, of nourishing others who are grandiose and omnipotent and stand in the center, a state where I'm altruistic, transcend myself for the benefit of others – would be impossible if not for twinship.

Twinship: rigidity in obeying social norms creates a situation of conformity and group uniformity. This strong normative stance in children has been argued to be a by-product of culture-gene coevolution because as social norms are an effective way of achieving conformity and cooperation among members of one's own group (Chudek & Henrich, 2011). Uniform and shared social norms make all the group's members equal, make everyone similar – twins – which creates a bridge enabling the transition between the two parts of the self: childhood (the self core) and social (SSC). Only when I feel like everyone else, I'm a twin like everyone else, and I feel that others are like me, they *are* me, can I behave toward others the same way I behave toward myself. This process only starts to exist from adolescence onward. During latency, as mentioned, the membrane between the two parts, childhood self and social self, each of which has a different state with different contents (willfulness and subordination), isn't fully functional. During latency, the psyche exists only in one part, the social self, and the process that enables the existence of this part is through the external-social reality. Existence in the social self requires the acceptance of shared social norms to form twinship. Without them, during the next stage, adolescence, the psyche won't be able to exist between the two parts of the self: childhood and social. The social norms create twinship, similarity, and equality. Latency prepares this infrastructure of twinship and social norms for the next developmental stage. Thus, social norms are vital for continued development. They are a matter of life and death. Children who don't accept the social norms and don't subordinate themselves to them cannot exist in society, and therefore cannot continue with their development, where they will nourish others and others will nourish them. They will be forced to live their lives in isolation and cut off from a nourishing and healthy social life.

Moral development according to the development in latency paradigm

Babies are born with an intuitive emotional sense of morality. Studies show this. Babies just a few months old prefer moral people. They distinguish between good and bad people (Tasimi, Johnson, & Wynn, 2017). Babies feel the suffering of others as their own suffering without distinguishing between themselves and others. They cry when other babies are crying. Infants who see other children crying try to help them. The intuitive moral sense is innate. It is as powerful as a drive or an instinct. It's a sense that doesn't follow the rules of education or logic and thought. It's a sense that doesn't distinguish between the self and other objects. This is the primary sense of justice that we all know, which awakens with a strong emotional force, independent of any external influence. A counter-force against the innate morality instinct is the psychological drives and needs, which are at the early stages of development. The grandiose, egocentric, solitary, omnipotent needs. These needs consolidate justice and morality in the children themselves. Children with a sense of justice and morality at the age of 2 to 3 years, when they feel that their egocentricity, possessiveness, and omnipotence have been harmed, can only stick to their own viewpoint and see justice as what is good for them. For example, a 2-year-old boy can run to help another boy who's crying and offer him a toy of his as a gesture of comfort. But when this same baby wants another beloved toy from the consoling boy, he won't be empathic anymore and will keep his toy to himself even when the baby resumes crying. In the same way, this boy won't agree to give up or lose to another when this is against his wishes and interests. This gap between moral understanding and moral behavior has been found in various studies (Smith, Blake, & Harris, 2013; Rizzo & Killen, 2016).

Children's morality is related to fulfilling psychological needs, the way the parents treat their infants in the early years, how gently and sensitively they provide for their children's needs (Govrin, 2014; Li, 2016). It's very important for children and adults to be capable of handling the fundamental moral dilemma of the impulse to do good and the impulse to do evil. When their needs for grandiosity, omnipotence, and object control are fulfilled, children can develop to the stage where in any dilemma between another's benefit and their own benefit, they will be capable of considering another's benefits. If these needs aren't satisfied, they can develop a strong need for control, possessiveness, and so on. This unfulfilled deficiency makes their ability to choose more limited. Children with deficiencies become adults who find it difficult in situations where they surrender control, possessiveness, grandiosity, and omnipotence. They will often be forced to behave immorally due to these deficiencies.

From birth up to the age of 5 or 6 years, children are cared for and educated by their parents. The education provided by the parents up to this age is based on the criteria and rules of the society in which the parents live. Five-year-old children who have received a good education at home and in kindergarten already internalize the moral rules their parents follow. They know well what's good and right to do according to these criteria. Usually, children who are educated according to our Western values will know, for example, that when they find a lost object, it's right and moral to return it to the person who lost it. Or when they see an act of violence, this will shock them.

Infantile morality in the self core – the superego: the superego is similar in operation to the drive, instinct part, and to part of the ego. It possesses particular powers that are forceful and inflexible. The morality of the superego is a very binding morality. It's not flexible at all. It is as sacred as divine laws. The parental moral system is assimilated into the entire psyche so it belongs to the psyche inseparably as part of the children's psyche. The process of assimilation and internalization is such that what is internalized becomes part of the thing in which it's assimilated or internalized, so that it can't be distinguished from it. The superego of the family moral system (which belongs to the society and is therefore called canonical morality) is a structure, a self-standing body that has a unique influence on the psyche. This is a moral essence whose quality is sealed within the self core. The morality in the self core moves mainly between two choices: behaving according to the superego's moral criteria, meaning according to the parents' moral upbringing, or acting in accordance with the drive forces of the early needs (omnipotence, grandiosity, egocentricity, and so on), according to what people want and feel entitled to. This is the conflict described in various religions between the impulse to do good and the impulse to do evil. But these two impulses face a real revolution during the next stage of development.

During latency, morality develops in a dimension that adds infinite complexity to every moral decision. Social morality doesn't belong to the real society in practice. This isn't a morality adapted only to the external reality of society. It's an intrapsychic moral quality that functions in accordance with the SSC's psychic system. This is the part of the self that operates in relation to the external reality, and in latency – according to what the classmates decide is moral. During latency, the gap that existed in the earlier stages between family morality and children's behavior disappears completely (Smith, Blake, & Harris, 2013). A transition occurs to morality in the function of the SSC, where social norms and behavior match and suit the group's norms (Abramson, Daniel, & Knafo-Noam, 2018; Rizzo & Killen, 2016; Schmidt, Svetlova, & Tomasello, 2016). The quality of morality in the SSC is relative, flexible, compromising; it's subject to changes, dependent on interests; it employs considerations of worthwhileness and rational thinking; it doesn't include components of emotion, instinct, and emotional identification. This morality can withstand the two other forces of the parts of the psyche: the drives of the id and the superego. Morality during latency is arbitrary and contains a dimension of separateness. It's a morality that enables flexibility and consideration of additional factors. An example of social morality is the moral law "Thou shall not murder". Social morality takes into consideration mitigating factors such as young age, insanity, and self-defense, so that the law becomes flexible. From adolescence onward, throughout adult life, people move between these two states:

1   Moral choice in the self core moral quality: being moral in accordance with the canonical family morality or adopting an egocentric position of satisfying needs and drives.
2   Moral choice between the self core moral quality and the SSC moral quality: between the family canonical morality and the social morality.

Self core morality is internal, personal, private morality. It's based on the values children acquire at home and in kindergarten. These values have the quality of superego. This is highly binding morality. Its instructions are as compulsory and valid as divine orders. The values of this morality are determined by the family, the community, and the nation. Thus, people whose family values encourage them to become a "shahid" (Muslim martyr) and those whose family values include "whoever saves one life saves the whole world" have the same quality of morality. Within the self core moral quality, these two moral values are equivalent. Young children absorb their parents' values, which are the values of their society, and these become the strongest part in the morality of the adult society that they will develop later. This is the most determining part. It possesses emotional, drive-based, instinctive, and intuitive force. This is also the conscience that guides and dictates our moral path. The moral choice within the self core can change through the morality in the SSC. The family canonical morality is rigid and uncompromising. It dictates moral choice in a deterministic and unconscious way, and therefore the ability to make a choice that doesn't follow it is very limited. But, surprisingly, during latency a morality develops that enables freedom of choice. This moral quality is relative and flexible according to social norms. Social morality adds to the canonical morality an essential dimension of awareness, relativity, flexibility, taking into consideration a range of factors and circumstances. These are the cases where leniency may apply. There are special cases that require us to take the circumstances into account and to deviate from rules and procedures.

The morality of the SSC can exist with preconditions of twinship. This quality of morality requires society to unite around shared social rules that create uniformity. A condition of similarity and uniformity among group members creates the important psychic state of "group twinship". Only group twinship can enable the psyche's transition between the two opposing psychic states: subordination and willfulness. When a society is in a condition of "group twinship", its members become mutually responsible. Latency teaches us that individuals who don't conform to their society's group twinship are subjected to an opposing, destructive, humiliating, depressing, ostracizing, and demeaning attitude. Such individuals are not removed from society; they continue to exist as members, but society does whatever it can to shock them and force them to adapt to it. Society has the tools for sensing even the slightest fake. Society can sense when individuals are pretending or when they're hiding their canonical morality and only apparently adapting themselves to society's norms. Even when they behave externally in accordance with all the social norms, society can still sense the moral genetic disposition that differentiates them from it. Individuals must commit themselves to the social morality in "group twinship" wholeheartedly; otherwise they are sentenced to social rejection.

Another point for discussion is the formation of the conscience. As noted earlier, the early stages build the conscience, with the end of the Oedipal stage sealing it and making it a subconscious moral compass. The conscience contains family and canonical morality, including religious and national values. Conscience is binary: things are either moral or immoral (the impulse to do good and the impulse to do evil). But even the conscience, despite being essentially finite and deterministic, contains complex and sometimes even contradictory contents. For example, when the parents disagree, such as when the father presents a flexible moral position while the mother presents a rigid position. Sometimes, the conscience can be sensitive in certain areas and apathetic in others. It can contain opposite morality in various areas. For instance, someone whose conscience is sensitive to the sanctity of human life and who helps people whenever possible, but who's apathetic to the suffering of animals. Or someone could be sensitive to human suffering, but show apathy to economic-business moral criteria.

As noted earlier, the conscience belongs to the childhood self part, and its foundation is physical, drive-based, instinctive, and emotional. It's shaped by powerful emotional experiences. Personal or family suffering sharpens moral sensitivity. For example, a girl who experiences a serious event of sickness or death will become morally sensitive to this type of suffering in adulthood. Early suffering enhances moral sensitivity to the same type of suffering in the future.

During the stage that follows latency, adolescence, when the passages between the self core and the SSC open in the membrane (whose role during latency is only blocking), transition between the two qualities becomes possible, and then we can continue discussing values with adolescents. In their independent way of constructing their own identities, adolescents seek spiritual guidance. Moral adults can choose between stubbornly sticking to the internal values of their conscience and acting flexibly according to social norms. They can find their way between these two moral qualities and reach compromises between them. In latency, in contrast, there is no choice whatsoever. Children must obey social norms. Disobeying society exacts an intolerable price from them. However, the social norms they obey have an infinite quality; they don't contain good and evil, and have no absolute, binding morality. Society's norms can change infinitely, according to the forces and currents in society. In contrast, the morality of conscience is personal, absolute, and binary: right or wrong, good or evil, moral or immoral. When adults follow social norms alone, they are denying or "betraying" the values of their conscience. They lose their "humanity". The conscience is in the internal, sacred part, which Winnicott calls "incommunicado": a hidden, secret core of the personality and the center of the inner life, which others can't access (Winnicott, 1964). The conscience grants inner meaning to moral choices. With social norms, there is often no personal meaning. People who follow their conscience when this opposes social norms may suffer serious social consequences. But from adolescence onward, people are capable of choosing to fight courageously in accordance with their conscience against the spirit of the era and the pressure of the regime and social trends. They can choose to act on the basis of their conscience and the values they received during early childhood and to oppose the values of a particular society.

The development of empathy during latency according to the self as a cell analogy

Empathy in the self core is founded upon interpersonal relationships (dyads or triads). The empathy is interpersonal, absolute, instinctive, and inseparable. A 2-day-old baby hearing the distress of another baby feels the same level of distress, without distinguishing between himself or herself and the crying baby (Hoffman, 2000). This is empathy of complete congruence between the two, without separateness. This is also the highest degree of empathy one can reach. It contains no doubt, no hesitation. The person feels the other as though it were himself or herself. This is the voice that makes people respond immediately to help others when hearing their distress, from an instinctive drive and absolute identification. Empathy in the self core is under the control of drives, demanding wishes, egocentricity-omnipotence, grandiosity, exhibitionism, exclusive control, and so on. In other words, empathy in the self core is interpersonal, emotional, unconditional, immediate, absolute, and complete. Children fully sense the suffering of others. But these two components are under the control of a one-dimensional, egocentric, grandiose vision. If a 5-year-old boy's friend cries in pain and sorrow, his best friend will respond with absolute and complete empathy, but if he cries because his best friend isn't letting him play with his toy, this won't necessarily make the boy give up his own toy in order to stop his best friend's sorrow ("I won't give it to him. Absolutely not. I don't care that he's crying. It's only mine and I don't want to!").

Empathy in the group SSC

This is empathy where children mercilessly break off previous interpersonal friendships and choose friendship relationships that are determined according to the hierarchy and that serve social interests. During latency, empathy is a social service – it operates in accordance with the group's values, status, and social hierarchy. It's interest-based, intellectual, controlled, manipulative, and strategic.

There's a paradox in the development of empathy. During the early developmental stages, in the childhood self, empathy is instinctive, uncontrolled, not separate. It awakens immediately in full, without any thought. The lack of separateness causes empathy to arise without hesitation, delay, thought, or control. Paradoxically, this is the highest level of human empathy, which we as cultured human beings aspire to reach: to rush immediately to help the suffering. However, at the early stages of development, empathy is limited by its egocentric and omnipotent quality. In other words, when moral young children are in a situation that threatens their central position, their control, or their omnipotence, they usually find it difficult to feel empathy toward others.

In contrast, empathy during latency is social. It's not emotional but intellectual, focused on social interests, hierarchy, and status. The other's distress is separate. This is a controlled, considered, strategic, and non-instinctive empathy. During latency, loyalty is social and group-focused rather than interpersonal. It's based on social interests. This empathy, too, is complex and even paradoxical: it doesn't threaten the grandiosity and omnipotence. Latency age children can surrender their egocentric, omnipotent, central place. In the struggle between the impulse to do good and the impulse to do evil, being moral toward others or fulfilling personal needs, latency age children can be moral and renounce their personal needs. Also, during latency, children are capable of understanding the other's viewpoint, so there is a higher capacity for empathy. However, paradoxically, during latency there is separation from others that means that identification with the other's suffering isn't automatic and there is no emotional identification with the other's suffering. Empathy during latency is motivated by intellectual, strategic social considerations.

To conclude, during latency, empathy in the self core is blocked. It lacks interpersonal loyalty, separateness, drives, egocentricity, omnipotence, and so on. It also lacks the innate, emotional instinctive morality. It doesn't contain the conscience of the superego, which is acquired during the Oedipal stage. All these things are blocked during latency. The implications of this understanding in reference to the "cruel" phenomena of latency, such as ostracism, bullying, and so on, is that *we can't use the methods that awaken empathy in the self core to treat these phenomena*, since this is a move that operates contrary to the nature of normative development in this age group, and there is no contact with this part.

Reasons for social rejection according to the developmental paradigm

According to the approach presented in this book, social rejection doesn't result from the socially rejected child's difficulty or disability. Nor does it result from a difficulty in the class dynamics. It's also not the result of faulty education or insufficient personal attention of the child's teacher. I argue that it's not even the product of failed parenting. Almost all the children who came to me for therapy had no disability and came from normative classes, from wonderful families with caring parents. Social rejection, according to the approach presented here, is completely normative. It occurs during latency, when the transition from the childhood self with the function of "willfulness" to the social self with the function of "subordination" is delayed. This transition isn't simple at all. It does occur in all children, but takes place subjectively in accordance with the emotional maturity, the fulfilling of the needs during the early stages, and innate traits. Social rejection requires all children to make this transition, even those who aren't sufficiently mature. Children whose needs during the early developmental stages were insufficiently fulfilled, for various reasons that don't necessarily imply failed parenting, find it difficult to transition to "subordination" during latency.

There are many socially rejected children. Almost all children experience social rejection at some stage, and this rejection is important because it teaches them, from experience, that they must be very attentive to society and that it's very desirable, for their own benefit and mental wellbeing, to turn their attention outward and develop sensitivity to the changes in social reality. The novel *Lord of the Flies* describes this process of one of the children's becoming aware of the dangers of social harm when he starts being alert like a hunting dog (Golding, 1954). Those who still, for various reasons, haven't made the transition to the social self with the function of "subordination" during latency, display a range of behaviors that don't suit the maturity level of their classmates. *Their immaturity means that they're still focused on themselves, seeking to present themselves and their traits and skills as unique, trying to display their abilities and superiority over the others.* These are children who split things between good and evil, experiencing themselves as good while the society of children is experienced as evil. Good in their eyes is based on the family, canonical moral values of the general society. The social norms of their classmates seem to them bad, stupid, valueless, and improper.

The differences between socially rejected children and those who are unpopular, popular, or class rulers in the experience of social rejection depend on the degree of maturity. Mature children, who have naturally transitioned to the maturity stage SSC, experience social rejection to the lightest degree. They can make a small error in perceiving the social norms, stereotypes, and correct handling of the class hierarchy and be mature enough to perceive this error immediately and adapt themselves, continuing on the developmental track of accurate social perception. The greater the frequency and power of rejection, the more the child is stuck in the self core and distant from transitioning to the SSC.

The delay in maturation that causes social rejection is often the result of the responsible adults' inability to release the child to develop independently within the autonomous society of children. Parents who are confident in their children will more easily release them to cope within the independent society of children. Most socially rejected children who come to me for therapy are children whose parents, for various reasons, protect them, are very close to them and involved in their lives, distrust the society of children to treat their children well, and don't trust their own children to manage in the social arena by themselves. In addition, they too, like their children, feel that the society of children doesn't suit their personality and their family behavior and values. Not releasing the children from their significant relationship with their parents to form relationships with the autonomous society of children causes the children to remain in the function of "willfulness" in the self core, which necessarily leads to loneliness and even social rejection. This situation is reinforced when parents who are devoted to their children discover that their children are rejected and ostracized. This makes them increase their connection and involvement in their children's lives. Many parents said to me: "It breaks my heart to see him lonely, so I go out with him, so at least he'll have somebody". This is a mistake. Their feeling of concern and compassion causes parents to keep their children in a state of "willfulness" in the self core, arresting their development.

Self psychology and social rejection according to the developmental paradigm

I argue that during latency the significant selfobject is the society of classmates. Kohut (1971, 1980, 1984) believed that the narcissistic development of the self was related to three axes, grandiosity, idealization, and twinship, and that it depends on the selfobject's responding to these three axes: a need for mirroring, a need for idealization, and a need for twinship. The need for mirroring is people's need to be visible, to be reflected in accordance with their developmental, chronological, and emotional stage and in accordance with their unique abilities and skills. The selfobject's fulfilling of this need leads to self-value, healthy ambitions, commitment, assertiveness, and achievement-orientation. The need for idealization is a need to connect and merge with the ideal, calm, and secure selfobject. Appropriate development on the idealization axis leads to the ability to self-calm and self-regulate, restraint, accepting frustration, and the ability to create and maintain a set of ideals, goals, and values. Twinship with the selfobject stems from the need to feel belonging and similarity, thus establishing the ability to feel a sense of belonging and connectedness, empathy, adopting social codes, and social skills. According to Kolke (2010), the development of the self doesn't occur in developmental stages, but throughout the person's life there is mobility between a state of "emergence" and a state of "dissolving".

> A state of permanent vibration between a finite immanent being, which I wish to term emergence, and an infinite transcendent coming-into-being, which I propose to call dissolving. [. . .] Emergence is a code word that I suggest for the physical state of things, whether the body we bear, with its sensations and desires, its pleasures and pains [. . .] the commitment to the reality of the personal self. [. . .] Dissolving is the term for man's ethics – his devotion to the world and everything in it. [. . .] The premise of the emergence-coping model [. . .] the need of a person's self to emerge requires an empathic matrix of a seeing selfobject, from which the person occurs as an existing and real individual being and in a complementary manner, the person's self's need for dissolving requires an empathic matrix of an idea selfobject that enables merging with everything that's beyond personal existence.
>
> (Kolke, 2010: 42)

I argue that this space exists in full from adolescence onward throughout life, while the two beings of emergence and dissolving develop up to latency. Emergence is similar to "willfulness" in the self core during the early stages of development, while dissolving is similar to the flexibility of the SSC. In adulthood, people move between these two experiences, and between them the membrane translates and compares these two experiences.

According to my approach, during latency, the society of classmates is the selfobject that fulfills the three axes described above. Satisfying these three axes during latency is of a different quality to the way they were fulfilled during early childhood. Children receive fulfillment of their grandiosity need by being prominent in their similarity to the other children in the group. Mirroring is provided by the society of children, and the children aren't outstanding in any particular quality or talent but by being similar to the society of children. When children perceive and follow the social norms, they adapt very accurately to the norm that makes everyone equal. The better a child adapts to the norm, the more popular he or she becomes, and those who are popular have their need for appreciation and admiration fulfilled. Accordingly, their self-image and self-confidence are strengthened. On the idealization axis, children during latency are nourished when they connect and merge with the selfobject of the society of children. They see the children, especially the "popular" ones, as admired, exceptional in their strengths, abilities, and talents. The children are able to obtain satisfaction on these two axes on the basis of "group twinship". When all the children are twins and similar to each other within the group according to the social norms, they receive nourishment on the axes of grandiosity and idealization. During latency, as described above, empathy is intellectual. This empathy can only be received in an existence of "group twinship". During latency, twinship is the most significant axis that enables the existence of the narcissistic system.

Kohut (1971) explained that when there's a deficiency in fulfilling the selfobject needs, this causes narcissistic damage. During childhood, this deficiency is expressed in sensations of low self-value, tension, anxiety, anger, and hostility. Such children may also develop negative self-view, a high spread of negative affect (emotion) in the structure of the self, frequent cognitive disorders, difficulties in performing achievement-related tasks, and intense negative emotions during their performance. Kohut believed that difficulties in the development of the three axes leads to disorders in the self, and if there is no healthy expression of grandiosity with mature goals, this causes detachment situations in relationships. People find it hard to maintain stability in their self-value or to set realistic goals and show empathy to others. The result is that people with damaged selves become defensive and critical. They fail, are motivated by negative emotions and pessimistic thoughts, and feel alienated and lonely (Banai, Mikulincer, & Shaver, 2005).

In other words, children who develop a deficiency in satisfying their selfobject needs become children with low self-image and low self-value, their self-efficacy will be low, and they'll perceive themselves as bad and weak people. They will be under-achievers and lack the motivation to succeed. In addition, they'll experience problems in interpersonal relationships, difficulties in emotional adaptation, in self-cohesion, and in emotional regulation. When there's a deficiency in the need for idealization, this creates developmental disruptions. Thus, when the selfobject fails in empathic provision of the baby's need for idealization, the baby's psychic structure is damaged and he or she may develop a disorder in emotional regulation (Kogan, 2013). During latency, all these deficiencies remain within the self core and are connected to the qualities of the childhood self (Fisher-Grafy, 2015). Where there is developmental delay, latency age children can carry these deficiencies into the social setting. Immature children, who still exist in the childhood self experience, can suffer when they demand from the society of children object control that wasn't fulfilled during their earlier stages. But during latency it's also possible to skip over these deficiencies. Latency enables the satisfaction of the selfobject needs in the new psychic dimension of the social self, and even children with deficiencies from earlier developmental stages can be nourished by the society of classmates. When they are in "group twinship" with the society of children they will obtain the nourishing described above.

To conclude, in my approach, during latency the quality of the three axes – grandiosity, idealization, and twinship – changes. Nourishing of these three axes in the self core is different from nourishing these three axes in the SSC.

References

Abramson, L., Daniel, E., & Knafo-Noam, A. (2018). The role of personal values in children's costly sharing and non-costly giving. *Journal of Experimental Child Psychology*, 165: 117–134.

Adolphs, R. (2003). Is the human amygdala specialized for processing social information? *Annals of the New York Academy of Sciences*, 985: 326–340.

Badenoch, B. (2016). A symphony of gifts from relational neuroscience: How understanding our embodied brains can support lives of hope & resilience. Retrieved from www.soundstrue.com/store/neuroscience-summit

Banai, E., Mikulincer, M., & Shaver, P.R. (2005). Selfobject needs in Kohut's self-psychology: Links with attachment, self-cohesion, affect regulation, adjustment. *Psychoanalytic Psychology*, 22(2): 224–260.

Bion W.R. (ed.) (1977). A theory of thinking. In: *Second Thoughts: Selected Papers on Psychoanalysis* (pp. 110–119). New York, NY: Jason Aronson.

Braams, B.R. & Crone, E.A. (2017). Longitudinal changes in social brain development: Processing outcomes for friend and self. *Child Development*, 88(6): 1952–1965.

Chudek, M. & Henrich, J. (2011). Culture-gene coevolution, norm-psychology, and the emergence of human prosociality. *Trends in Cognitive Sciences*, 15(5): 218–226.

Durkheim, E. (2008). *The Elementary Forms of Religious Life*. Trans. M.S. Cladis & C. Cosman. Oxford: Oxford University Press.

Fisher-Grafy, H. (2015). *Socially Rejected Children*. Tel Aviv: Resling [Hebrew].

Freud, A. (1936). The ego and the mechanisms of defence. In *The Writings of Anna Freud* (Vol. 2). New York: International Universities Press.

Freud, S. (1905). Three essays on the theory of sexuality. In *The Standard Edition of the Complete Psychological Works of Sigmund Freud, Vol. VII (1901–1905): A Case of Hysteria, Three Essays on Sexuality, and Other Works.* Trans. J. Strachey. New York: W. W. Norton & Company; 1st edition (March 17, 1976).

Frith, C.D. (2007). The social brain? *Philosophical Transactions of the Royal Society of London Series B, Biological Sciences*, 362: 671–678.

Golding, W. (1954). *Lord of the Flies.* London: Faber and Faber.

Govrin, A. (2014). The ABC of moral development: An attachment approach to moral judgment. *Frontiers of Psychology*, 5: 6.

Hoffman, M.L. (2000). *Empathy and Moral Development: Implications for Caring and Justice.* New York: Cambridge University Press.

Hofmann, S.G. & Doan, S.N. (2018). *The Social Foundations of Emotion: Developmental, Cultural, and Clinical Dimensions.* Washington, DC, US: American Psychological Association.

Kogan, C. (2013). On the question of the good in man: Between superego and idealization. *Sichot*, 28(1): 60–66. [Hebrew].

Kohut, H. (1971). *The Analysis of the Self.* New York: International Universities Press.

Kohut, H. (1980). *Self Psychology and the Humanities: Reflections on a New Psychoanalytic Approach.* New York: W. W. Norton & Co.

Kohut, H. (1984). *How Does Analysis Cure?* Chicago: University of Chicago Press.

Kolke, R. (2010). The contribution of the psychology of the self to the spiritual dimension in psychoanalysis: Reflections on *Self Psychology and the Humanities* by Heinz Kohut. *Ma'arag*, 1: 263–279. [Hebrew].

Li, S. (2016). A mechanism for gratitude development in a child. *Early Child Development and Care*, 186(3): 466–479.

Neisser, U. (1988). Five kinds of self-knowledge. *Philosophical Psychology*, 1(1): 35–59.

Ornstein, A. (1986). Models for transmuting internalization. In *Progress in Self Psychology*, edited by A. Goldberg (pp. 129–132). New York: Guilford.

Rizzo, M.T. & Killen, M. (2016). Children's understanding of equity in the context of inequality. *British Journal of Developmental Psychology*, 34: 569–581.

Rochat, P. (2009). *Others in Mind: Social Original of Self-Consciousness.* New York, NY, US: Cambridge University Press.

Rutland, A. & Killen, M. (2017). Fair resource allocation among children and adolescents: The role of group and developmental processes. *Child Development Perspectives*, 11(1): 56–62.

Schmidt, M.F.H., Svetlova, M.J., & Tomasello, J.M. (2016). Children's developing understanding of legitimate reasons for allocating resources unequally. *Cognitive Development*, 37: 42–52.

Smith, C.E., Blake, P.R., & Harris, P.L. (2013). I should but I won't: Why young children endorse norms of fair sharing but do not follow them. *PLoS One*, 8(3): 59510.

Symington, J. & Symington, N. (1996). *The Clinical Thinking of Wilfred Bion.* Abingdon, UK: Routledge.

Tasimi, A.T., Johnson, M.K., & Wynn, K. (2017). Children's decision making: When self-interest and moral considerations conflict. *Journal of Experimental Child Psychology*, 161: 195–201.

Winnicott, D. (1964). *The Child the Family and the Outside World*. London: Pelican Books.

4   Envelopes

An individual therapy method

The Envelopes Therapy method was described in detail in my book *Socially Rejected Children* (Fisher-Grafy, 2015). Here I will briefly describe the method and present its updated version. The method described here promotes the understanding that the socially rejected child exists in the function of "willfulness" in the childhood self and finds it difficult to transition to existing in the SSC in the function of "subordination". A real change occurs already during the first session with the child, when the existence of the subordination function is enabled within the willfulness function. This allows flexibility within the willfulness function and starts to change the child's attitude toward social issues.

The stages of the Envelopes Therapy method: after a preliminary meeting with the parents, the child arrives for the first session.

First session with the child

1   Receiving the child warmly, with a smile. Therapist: "Hello! How are you?"
2   The therapist asks the child to rank his or her social position in the class from one to ten. Next, the child is asked to note the position he or she wishes to reach, and finally the amount of effort he or she is willing to invest in obtaining this position.
3   The child lists all the children in his or her class who are: friends/enemies/just classmates, and the therapist records these data in three columns on a page.
4   The list is cut up into notes with one name on each, and the notes are sorted into piles on top of three envelopes on which the child writes "friends", "enemies", and "just classmates".
5   When the notes with children's names are placed visibly on top of each envelope, the child is asked to choose a note with one name whose location in the envelopes he or she wants to change.

6   The note the child chooses is placed on a fourth envelope, called "star of the week". The child is asked to give a detailed description of the chosen child. This constitutes the diagnosis of the social barrier, and so it's recorded verbatim by the therapist, without interrupting the child's speech. It's important to note that during the first two sessions, the choice of the first two notes constitutes projection, focused on two issues: first, the child's ideal self. This means that the child is describing another child whom he or she considers ideal, thus sketching the patient's desired and preferred qualities. Second, the areas where the barrier to social integration is located.

7   The child is asked to describe a situation that happened to him or her with the chosen child. This is the important part of the therapy. The cases the children describe almost always present the clash between the children's personal will and the chosen child's will, which represents the social norms.

After the children present the case, the therapist sums it up in simple and clear terms: *You wanted X and the class group wants Y.* The children exist in the childhood self function where they willfully, rigidly, and uncompromisingly uphold the family values and rules and the canonical moral rules. They encounter the class's social rules, which they consider arbitrary and contrary to their moral instinct. Let's take a look at two case studies presenting the first session and the moment of confrontation between the willful childhood self and subordination to the class group's will in the social self, and see how to handle the confrontation using the tools arising from the developmental paradigm.

The first session with Andy

THERAPIST: "Hello, Andy. How are you?"

ANDY: "Good".

T: "Great. Please rank your social position in the class between one and ten".

A: "Three".

T: "What position do you want to reach?"

A: "Seven".

T: "How much effort are you willing to invest in this?"

A: "A lot".

T: "Please tell me the names of all the children who are your friends".
   He lists the names, and the therapist writes them down.

T: "Now tell me the names of the children who are your enemies".
   He lists the names, and the therapist writes them down.

T: "Now tell me the names of children who are just classmates, neither friends nor enemies".

He lists the names, and the therapist writes them down.

T: "Choose one name out of all the names with whom you want to change your situation, and place it on the envelope marked 'star of the week'".

Andy chooses the name Rob.

T: "Describe Rob to me".

A: "He's taller than me, among the tallest in the class. We have four boys in the soccer league, and he's one of them. When we play and I take the ball from him, he shouts at me. Then all the boys start shouting at me too. They also laugh at me and say I talk like a girl".

Analysis of the chosen boy, Rob: Andy himself is short. For him, this is a social barrier. Another barrier is not belonging to the boys who play league soccer. Andy doesn't accept the class hierarchy and takes the ball away from the boys' "king". He exists in a situation where he wants appreciation and admiration of his abilities and prominent achievements. He also doesn't accept the norm of the boys' stereotype that boys don't talk much.

Andy finishes his description, and the therapist asks him to describe Rob further:

T: "What sort of student is he?"

A: "When we work in pairs, everyone wants to be with him, he's popular. We have a class group of popular kids, and then there are the most popular. They say he's a great student and lots of boys want to be with him in soccer too".

T: "Now tell me about something that happened to you with Rob".

A: "During the break we had to be in the classroom and they showed videos. I was watching and then two boys came up to me and one of them asked me to punch him. I asked how, and he said 'on the shoulder'. I didn't know what to do, because I'm a peace-loving boy. So, I gave him a weak punch on the shoulder and he started imitating me and laughing at me. It was really bad. He started whining like a girl, and then I got annoyed and walked up to him, shoving aside everyone who was in my way. I'm sorry that I hurt Rob, he's innocent. I just pushed him. He tried to protect himself. Then all the boys started laughing at me and teasing, 'Watch out for Andy, he's really strong!' Then they laughed at me and called me 'gay' and said I was the weakest, and I really am weak because I don't like hitting people. I prefer to solve everything with words. So, I started crying and lay down on the floor and cried really hard. I was offended. It was a stinky situation. The teacher investigated, and said that now they're thinking how to handle them".

T: "So, the boys asked you to behave in a really immoral way. They demanded that you hit someone, something you are absolutely unable and unwilling to do. You're a peace-loving boy. You don't like hitting. Your parents and teachers and I really appreciate your morality. We all want to be peace-loving. But the boys in your class, for them morality is completely different. They hit each other, right?"

A: "Yes".

T: "Now, I'm going to explain to you what happens at your age, only at your age. There's 'I' and there's 'the class group'. I want one thing and the class group wants something else. OK?"

A: "OK".

T: "Everything that happens in class happens between these two, the I and the class group. Each of them has advantages and disadvantages. OK?"

A: "OK".

T: "The advantage of acting according to my own will, which means remaining willful and not compromising, that is not hitting other people. It's important to me, not to give in. Not to bend. To hold onto my personal morality, which is the rightest and best. And of course, you're right to behave this way. We want our society not to be violent, we want everyone to live in peace and not to hurt each other, and certainly not to hit each other and punch each other. So, it's important to follow my own will and not to hurt others. If I follow my will, I'll feel good about myself, because I'll be moral and good. And other people will also think I'm good and moral, and this is what I want people to think about me. I don't want them to think I'm bad and behave terribly. So, if I follow my will, I'll feel calm and whole because I follow my personal principles and behave well and morally".

T: "But, what's the disadvantage? The thing is that the class group won't accept any rule except its own rules. If you don't follow these rules, they exclude you from society. And then, when you're excluded from society it feels terrible. Because you see everyone together, and you're on the outside, you're not in the social life of the class group".

T: "Now, let's see what happens when you follow the class group's will and rules, rather than my own will and morality. If you follow the class group's way, it accepts you and you belong socially. This is the best feeling in the world. You feel good about yourself, comfortable, calm, you can concentrate on your studies, live comfortably. But, this involves a very big concession, since it's almost impossible to do this. It's something that's very hard to do. It's almost impossible to give up our will".

The therapist uses the words "we" and "our" so as not to leave the child alone in facing this dilemma.

T: "We can't give up. After all, it's our conscience. How can we give up our personal will? How can we give up our conscience? How can we give up being good and become bad? It's simply impossible".

The therapist reflects for the children their current situation where they are unable, due to still existing in the childhood self and the function of willfulness, to exist in a condition of concession that suits the condition of subordination in the social self part.

T: "Understand?"

A: "Yes".

T: "So, what can we do? It's all up to you. You're holding the reins and you decide at each moment which way you'll turn, to 'I' or to 'society'. In each situation, you have to check what suits you. How much are you able to bend and surrender your personal will. If you feel that you can't, that's fine! You're allowed to keep your own personal will. But you'll be aware from today onward that you chose this option. And you'll be aware that the price and the disadvantage is that society rejects you and doesn't accept you. Society rejects you not because it finds anything wrong with you or because you're unworthy or unloved. It rejects you just because you chose not to subordinate yourself and obey it. It's important to know that this is in your hands".

A: "So, what's better?"

T: "It's better for you to turn to society. Because while it will be difficult to give up your personal will, you'll become popular and belong and this will make you feel calm and help you continue with your life. But if you feel that you can't surrender to society, that's fine too. Because whenever you choose your personal will and society reacts with rejection, that's not so terrible at all. Because these things change rapidly. One moment you accept society's will and you're popular, and the next moment you don't accept society's will and you're rejected again, and the next moment you accept society's will again and they accept you back immediately. You really don't need to worry about this. At your age, things change very quickly. And you don't have to be afraid. The moment you subordinate yourself, they'll accept you back".

A: "I understand. I have to choose between 'I' and 'society'. Is there only one possibility? No option of both?"

T: "No. It's either one or the other. You can't combine both of them".

A: "Oh! I get it! It's like oil and water. You have to choose one of them".

T: "Yes, you can't both give a punch and also make it weak".

A: "If you try to do both, it's worse than just going along with what I want. Because it's like mixing vinegar with drinking soda powder, like Coca-Cola and Mentos. It creates an explosion. If I do both, give a punch but a weak one, the boys are most cruel towards me. If I'd told them: 'No!

I don't hit', they would have been less cruel. And if I'd punched hard, I would have belonged among them and they would have appreciated me".

T: "That's right".

The first session with Sophie

Let's skip the first part of the session and start at the core of the first session, the choice of the name of the child with whom the patient wants to change their relationship. Sophie chose a note with a girl's name and described her as follows.

SOPHIE: "She's like me, also gets offended, shy, competitive, smart, and lacking self-confidence".

Sophie is describing the social barriers she faces: offended, shy, competitive, smart, and lacking self-confidence. In her class, it transpires later, the popular girls are poor students, in particular the "class queen", and find it hard to accept Sophie's smartness and academic success. Later during therapy, after her social situation had improved, Sophie's main difficulty became explicit. A strong grandiose need expressed in high competitiveness, which she suppressed herself through shyness and lack of self-confidence. Sophie continued describing the girl she named:

S: "She behaves well".

Behaving well according to the adults' standards indicates, according to Kohlberg (Colby & Kohlberg, 2010), a very low moral developmental level, where children are moral in order to appear good to adults, when in fact the higher moral level is adapting to social norms.

S: "She's on the border between classmate and friend. She sits next to me. I'd like to become better friends with her if we could strengthen our connection".

Sophie is still in the childhood self function and prefers close interpersonal relationships with one good friend.

S: "The relationship is good. There's no problem between us, but I want more, to strengthen the relationship".

T: "What's missing in your relationship?"

S: "We should meet more and talk, play together during breaks, to be with her all the time, even in the afternoon".

To expand understanding and diagnosis, the therapist repeats the words Sophie used to describe the chosen girl and asks for further explanations.

T: "You said she gets offended. What does that mean?"

S: "She's offended when she loses because she's competitive. She's friends with the class queen. I want to be friends with her but not with the class queen".

T: "Why?"

S: "Because the class queen tells me what to do, who to be friends with and who not. I won't listen to her. I'll talk to whoever I want. She tells me when we're together not to include others, and I'm not willing to do this. I want to include everyone. That everyone in the class will be friends with everyone, because that way there's less fighting and you can get to know more children. Most of the fights are with the boys. I don't like it when there's shouting. There are children who bully and they want to drag me into it. I'm tempted to do something back to them, but I don't want to do this. Some children really bully other children, call them names, laugh at them. They often laugh at certain children and want to pull everyone along with them. I don't like being pulled along".

T: "Why don't you like being pulled along?"

S: "Just because everyone does it doesn't make it OK. The problem is that children have to do it to be with everyone. Children don't care. They keep laughing at other children and I won't accept it. But the problem is that I end up alone because the girls won't play with me and hurt me, and then I can't concentrate on studying, and I always feel lonely and wonder what to do".

Next, the therapist presents the two essences in this age: first, I and my will, and second, the class group and its will. Being with my will includes: private, canonical, and family morality, and the wish to be friends with one interpersonal friend. Being with the class group includes flexibility and subordination to social norms and also the quality of class group friendship.

T: "You're right. There's a class group of children who don't behave morally and you're not willing to behave like them. You're not willing to laugh at others, you're not willing to exclude some of the children and hurt them, you're not willing to bully children, call them names. You hate fighting, and you want to be best friends with the girl you particularly like".

T: "Your qualities and values are simply wonderful. Adults really appreciate your values and behavior. But at your age, the class group has lots
of power. The class group can decide on values and behavior that are
completely opposite from our wonderful values. Now, we have two possibilities and we choose which way to take".

T: "Each way has advantages and disadvantages. If we choose our personal
will and follow our values and morality, which are admirable, even
when we're adults, this makes us feel good about ourselves. We won't
be pressured by anything and can simply be ourselves. The disadvantage
is that the class group won't accept anyone not obeying its rules and they
reject whoever doesn't behave that way and treat them terribly, and then
we feel bad all the time and think about being lonely, and it disturbs our
concentration on our studies. If we choose the class group, the disadvantage is that we have to make a painful concession and sometimes we feel
that we simply can't, we're not willing to make this concession. On the
other hand, the advantage is that the class group accepts us and then we
don't feel any pressure, any loneliness, and we're calm and able to do
things calmly, like concentrate on our studies".

The case studies of these two children present the following idea: children
who are socially rejected are still, usually, in the early developmental function of the childhood self, which includes: willfulness, grandiosity, omnipotence, interpersonal friendship, and family morality. Rejected children are
not ready for the transition to the social self, and this creates the social
difficulties. The therapeutic question is how to move them into the social
self function when they're not yet mature for this stage. It's not possible to
awaken and increase their identification and empathy for others. It's impossible to move them into the social self function when they're still in a condition of willfulness.

The only way to help them is to cause them to get out of their psychic
position and say: "All the adults, parents, and teachers would agree with
you that your will is correct and logical". This statement, adapted to the
patient's psychic position, is not in any way untrue. Indeed, usually the children's personal will expresses adult morality (for example: nonviolence).

At the next stage, we move them into a position where they can choose
the way that's right for them. Their choice in this situation is still within the
function of willfulness, but it enables them to adapt to the general social
function of subordination. We tell them:

You can choose. You hold the reins. You're the one who decides which
way to turn. There are two directions and you alone choose the direction that suits you.

The choice allows the children a maneuvering space that reduces the pressure and gives them the sense of unique, personal control that suits their willful function.

Each choice has advantages and disadvantages. The advantages of the two ways are wonderful, and the costs of the two ways are very hard. One way is to follow your will, which is a wonderful will that the adults appreciate. It's most fun and calming to follow my own will and feeling. Not to concede it. To go the way in which I wholeheartedly believe. But the cost is that the society of children in the class only accepts those who follow their way, and they reject those who don't follow their way, and it's very hard to accept rejection. We're very miserable when this happens to us, and it hurts us a lot.

The other way is to follow society. This way also exacts a high, difficult price because it forces us to do something that's almost impossible: to give up our personal will, belief, and values. We know how right our will is, and how much our parents and teachers appreciate us when we follow it. The advantage of this choice is that the society of children accepts us into it and then we feel calm and happy and can continue our lives feeling a wonderful sense of popularity and social belonging.

In the following sessions (and no more than two or three sessions are required), the children act on this understanding, and their social situation improves. Sometimes, after their social position improves, some patients require long-term therapy, mainly to compensate for early deficiencies.

References

Colby, A. & Kohlberg, L. (2010). *The Measurement of Moral Judgment* (Vol. 1). Cambridge, UK: Cambridge University Press. (First published in 1987).
Fisher-Grafy, H. (2015). *Socially Rejected Children*. Tel Aviv: Resling [Hebrew].

5   Teacher interventions for social difficulties

In order to provide a suitable response to difficulties within the school system (social rejection, negative social norms) let's briefly present the foundations of the developmental understanding presented earlier:

Latency is a developmental stage when the children's psyche exists in the social part of the self. As such, the social reality in the class is an inseparable part of the intrapsychic existence. Just as infants who reach motor maturity for walking start to walk around in a world that is walkable to them, so children during latency, when they reach social maturity, start to exist in a social world. Therefore, the social reality during elementary school, which includes social rejection, social hierarchy, social norms, and the authority of class rulers, is inherent in the intrapsychic developmental stage. *In fact, every action, behavior, or statement of schoolchildren should be seen as expressing the children's social self.* These are proper, normative, and even essential developments for this developmental stage, latency.

This premise is important, because it sees all these phenomena as part of the healthy range of normative development. This is in contrast with the current treatment of them as belonging to the realm of difficulties, failings, and psychopathologies.

Now, let's list the variables in the developmental paradigm presented in the previous chapter, and build upon them a school intervention approach that is appropriate to the stage:

- During latency, which arrives after the Oedipal stage, the psychic functions of the previous stages are blocked: omnipotence, grandiosity, egocentrism, object control, and the superego that includes the canonical family morality.
- During latency, the society of classmates becomes a selfobject more significant than the selfobject of parents/kindergarten teachers/teachers, from whom the children separate.

- The classmates' society selfobject functions autonomously. It has internal authority. It is dictated by social hierarchy, social norms, stereotypes, and so on.
- The children receive grandiose nourishing from their classmates' society for being prominent in their similarity to the group's behavior. The more a child is "like everyone else", the greater his or her acceptance and esteem among the children.
- The children's idealism is nourished when they admire and want to belong with the class rulers and popular children. These popular children and class rulers are perceived by latency age children as admired, powerful figures who should be followed and imitated. The experience of belonging to the popular group gives a sense of connection with a superior person, and this strengthens the feeling of self-confidence, self-value, and a good sense of self. By merging with the selfobject of their classmates, children feel self-confident and confident in their abilities.
- Children receive twinship nourishing through the class norms. Class norms create twinship similarity among all the class's children. Creating a condition of twinship enables nourishing. During latency, children exist in the social part of the psyche in a state of subordination, involving giving nourishment rather than receiving it. Thus, accepting the social norms is very important for psychic development. Accepting the social norms creates twinship, which enables nourishing. This is the reason that the social norms shouldn't be fought, but supported.

The developmental task of the latency stage

The developmental task during the latency stage is the transition from a state of willfulness, omnipotence, egocentricity, receiving nourishing, to a state of subordination, adaptation to society, surrender, providing nourishing. This transition is possible through a process of twinship and unity, homogeneity, and consolidation. Achieving a state of twinship ("equivalence of form") occurs through social norms and social hierarchy.

Social norms and social hierarchy

The importance of social norms for development during latency

As we have seen, social norms play a critical role in the transition from the childhood self to the social self and are essential for continued development. They are also an important component in determining the autonomy of the class group. They are vital in establishing the social hierarchy and in creating the group identity. In terms of moral development, social norms possess great importance in adding a layer to the process of making a moral decision. Without the social norms, moral decisions would be made with the absolute quality of the rigid and uncompromising superego. Social norms add to the moral decision the dimensions of relativity, flexibility, contingency, and consideration for particular cases and situations.

The great pressure on the children to obey social norms increases the power of relative morality and gives it equivalence to the superego's absolute-canonical morality. Only equivalence between these two separate moral qualities enables the freedom of moral choice between the two, which starts to occur from adolescence onward. Without the increased pressure to obey social norms, relative morality would be unable to maintain the choice between two equal forces.

The qualities of the social norms that contribute to development during latency

The two main qualities of the social norms are: 1. arbitrariness; and 2. rapid change. These two qualities are helpful and essential for intrapsychic development during latency – the transition to psychic subordination. The relative dimension of morality requires the norms, unlike the canonical moral values, to be arbitrary and sometimes even to lack moral justification. Obeying them doesn't stem from internal identification with their emotional, human value, or from an internal need for justice. Their developmental role necessitates their arbitrariness. Thus, the emphasis shifts from the content of the norm to external-social factors, such as social hierarchy. The reason for the social norm of wearing a certain shoe brand or a pink scarf, for example, has no importance. No particular brand has any significant justification, but children still insist strongly on obeying this norm. They will demand that their parents buy them a specific shoe brand or a scarf in a particular shade of pink, purely due to their commitment to following social norms. It's not the content of the norm that matters to the children, but social interests like being accepted, receiving social approval and appreciation, and progressing in the hierarchy.

The rapid changes in social norms appear, for instance, in frequent changes in the types of game the whole class plays, or items of clothing or brands. The rapid and arbitrary changes of social norms contribute to the developmental task of transitioning from willfulness to subordination. As the Talmud describes: "A person should always be soft like a reed, and he should not be stiff like a cedar" (Babylonian Talmud, Taanit 20a). The cedar, like the canonical morality, is upright, fixed, and steadfast. The reed bends and moves with the wind. Subordination requires moving with the wind, observing the currents, who's in charge and dictating norms, what's being dictated, how we should behave now and in the near future. These qualities of arbitrariness and rapid change improve and enhance the flexibility of subordination, sensitivity to perceive and grasp the norms and subtleties of social changes. The norms, which are usually not phrased in words, melt away when perceived or touched. The moment they become defined and formulated, they quickly dissipate and get replaced by new norms. One child described it brilliantly:

> By the time I notice which computer game everyone is playing and becoming excellent at, and by the time I start playing it and getting good at it, everyone has already moved on to another game, gaining so many points that I'll never catch up with them.

Through the threat and fear of remaining outside the group of children, not belonging, and even being socially rejected, children develop sharp feelers for perceiving the social norms and adapting themselves to them quickly.

Dominant social norms reject the adult morality

An important development during latency, as mentioned, in the transition from the childhood self to the social self, is the change from willfulness to subordination. The existence of the individual's self in a state of subordination requires the power of the group of classmates to which the individual can be subordinate. Various psychological theories, as we saw earlier, grant importance to the society of classmates during latency (Winnicott, 1962; Freedman, 1996). When parents and teachers strictly uphold moral values and remain dominant in children's lives during latency, they don't enable them to transition to the desired psychic state for this developmental stage, which requires social autonomy and strong control of social hierarchy and norms. Children must act independently according to social norms that enable the development of a relative, variable morality that depends on social factors.

As we saw above, studies have found that children during latency obey social norms and pay little attention to adult morality. The adults must understand that rejection of the morality they represent is essential, and that when they fight the children's social norms and struggle forcefully to maintain the adults' morality as dominant, they are harming the children's development. For example: in the fifth grade, only the popular children are invited to a birthday party. The homeroom teacher fights this norm and offers the children only two options: inviting all the children in the class, or inviting a very small number of children (two to four). As described earlier, in such cases children tend to behave externally as obeying the adults' authority. Indeed, on the overt level they will invite either all the girls or just two or three friends. But under the surface, in the normative developmental space, they will stick to their social norm and the hierarchy that states they should invite the popular children they prefer. When teachers succeed in suppressing the hierarchy, the group of children finds alternatives in situations where the hierarchy can be reinforced. *The purpose of strengthening the hierarchy, as argued above, is creating a uniformity of norms that paves the way to twinship, enabling the transition from willfulness to subordination.* Thus, the group of children must reject the adults' morality; it must maintain the hierarchy that establishes the uniformity of norms that enables twinship, which, in turn, facilitates the transition from willfulness to subordination.

Lability of social norms, social hierarchy, and stereotypes

Three factors, social norms, stereotypes, and social hierarchy, support creating uniform shared norms. The purpose, as mentioned, is to create uniformity that facilitates the transition from being nourished to providing nourishing, and from willfulness to subordination. It requires all the children to behave according to the social norms, completely identically. The stereotypes support uniformity. The division between boys and girls during latency and the gender stereotypes make it easy to create a shared system of norms for each gender separately. Separating the boys and girls is essential for constructing a set of norms of similarity among the boys, distinct from the girls. The social hierarchy supports obeying social norms, and thus contributes to uniformity. Children obey the popular children and the class rulers, follow the dictated norms, and thus the group of children becomes uniform.

But here we encounter the great developmental challenge children must face. While the class uniformity is created by similar behavior following the social norms, this uniform behavior is not flexible. Everyone must obey and follow it strictly, without any option for individual variation. All the rest of the factors, norms, hierarchy, and stereotypes, are labile and constantly changing. The dependence of these factors on each other also contributes to the instability and lability. A change in one is connected to changes in the other factors. Thus, any small change in one factor changes all the factors. One day the stereotype of girls is to "be weak" and scream in alarm when they encounter a bug, and the next day being weak is related to physical weakness. A rejected girl can advance in the hierarchy if she adapts herself to the changing stereotype.

It seems to parents and adults that their child's fate is sealed when he or she is "stuck" at a low social status. But this is not the case during latency.

A girl in a low position in the hierarchy makes friends with girls higher up the hierarchy, and thus progresses. A girl high in the hierarchy who opposes the class queen drops to a lower rank in the hierarchy. If the class queen supports the parents' morality in a certain situation, she can be replaced instantly. If rejected children accept the social norms and the hierarchy in which someone else is in the center and at the top of the hierarchy, immediately their social status improves. In other words, the children exist within a fluctuating system of various social factors that are interdependent and that influence each other. The developmental challenge during latency is very difficult and even seems impossible, but for the mature children it's amazingly natural: creating group uniformity, establishing it somehow while many variables keep shifting, in a system that's constantly fluctuating. Children, as members of the children's group, are required to move in accordance with the group's movement. For this to happen, they must let go of the perception system appropriate to the childhood self, where they are the main recipient of the events, and to move with the entire group through the range of changes that occur in it. The multiplicity of changing factors contributes to the group's movement, like a school of fish moving with the changing currents.

Enforcing social norms through social sanctions

As mentioned in the previous chapter, the children's group has a system that enforces social norms. It has a system for observing, warning, judging, and finally sentencing. The sentence for not accepting and obeying the social norms is usually cruel and includes social rejection in all its vicious manifestations. The main purpose of social rejection is to destabilize, shock, and threaten the rejected child's existential security. The socially rejected child feels great distress that can be compared to fear of psychic castration. The enforcement system and the cruel sanction of social rejection serve an important role in the developmental task of latency. It requires children, due to the pressure it exerts, to be in a constant state of preparedness to hear the shot of rejection whistling past. Children are entirely focused on perceiving changes in the norms, the hierarchy, the stereotypes, knowing that even the slightest inaccuracy could lead to the threatening shot. They are constantly alert. They have to balance a system that is subject to the pressures of dynamic, unstable factors. On the one hand, they are pulled by the developmental drive to belong socially, and for this they have to keep moving in complete correspondence with the forces that move the group: norms, hierarchy, and stereotypes. On the other hand, they have to keep their balance among all the changes and lability of the social forces and currents, and to remain constantly completely identical to the group, when any failure of inaccuracy, any lack of identity with the group, or any unique expression could lead to the deterring shock of social rejection. Therefore, teachers and parents must understand how complicated the developmental task of latency is and take care not to add obstacles that only confuse the growing environment. By fighting to suppress the enforcement of social sanctions, imposing severe punishments on those who apply the sanctions and follow social norms that the parents can't accept, and thus preaching the canonical morality, they are only enhancing an individualism that opposes the normative developmental processes and causing a delay in development.

Social norms, social hierarchy, stereotypes, and prejudices

Studies examining the phenomenon of social rejection during latency have attempted to understand it within a wider context as belonging to other serious social phenomena such as: prejudices, racism, gender, and stereotypes. These studies checked what influenced children to apply social rejection to different races or genders. According to these studies, children are rejected because they are of an "inferior" ethnicity or race about which a prejudice exists, or from a low socio-economic status (for a review of research literature on this issue, see Fisher-Grafy, 2015). According to the approach presented here, race and gender have no importance in social rejection during latency. Discrimination in the general society differs from the phenomenon of social rejection during latency. Even if statistics indicate such a tendency, the cause for it is different. Teachers, parents, and even the children themselves are mistaken to attribute the rejection of certain children to their belonging to an "inferior" ethnicity or socio-economic status.

As we have noted, the society of children must create uniformity and similarity between all its members. They create this through the social norms. Stereotypes and gender are factors that enable a division that makes it easier to create shared norms. It's easier to construct and present a social norm of weakness based on a stereotype of weak girls and to establish a social norm of the girls regarding their weakness. Such a norm can't coexist with the boys' stereotype, which is the opposite: being strong and brave. The stereotypes and the gender division help create the common denominator to establish uniformity in social norms. What is special about latency is that both the stereotypes and the gender division are unrelated to social class and discrimination. The girls are the ones who determine the norm whereby they are weak, easily startled, and delicate. The social hierarchy, which is important for operating the changing system of social norms, is what determines the hierarchy of stereotypes, gender, and prejudice. In other words, the girls in the popular group decide that girls of their level must be from a high socio-economic status. Girls from a low socio-economic status in the class can't belong to the popular group. They feel that they have a lower social status and that they receive unequal and discriminatory treatment. But from developmental terms, it's not the socio-economic status that decided the social hierarchy. A girl who is attentive to the changing social norms; adapts her clothing, speech, and behavior; and is subordinate to the class queen, won't be socially rejected even if her ethnicity is considered "inferior" or if she comes from a low socio-economic status. For example: the class queen says, "I went abroad during the vacation". None of the other girls in the class has been abroad, but they can support her statement by saying: "It's fun to go abroad!" and so on. In other words, behavior adapted to the social norms is what determines the social hierarchy. The stereotypes don't determine the norms and the hierarchy. Quite the opposite. The social hierarchy establishes the social norms. The stereotypes are decided within the social norms. A stereotype of an ethnicity or race is influenced by adaptation to the social norm, and once such children adapt themselves to the social norms, the hierarchy changes. For example: a girl from a low socio-economic status, from a low social class, who adapts herself to the social norms and subordinates herself to the class queen will improve her rank in the hierarchy. The class queen says she bought a certain brand of jeans (during latency, the brands aren't necessarily expensive), and the girl takes an interest in the experience of buying this brand, appreciates and admires this purchase. Her act of sharing brings her closer to the hierarchy and the norms and lets her belong to the group of girls. Of course, she could also buy the same brand and immediately belong to the group. The most significant factor is subordination to the social norms and the hierarchy that establishes them. If children accept and obey the social norms and subordinate themselves to those higher in the hierarchy, they can change their status, regardless of stereotypes and prejudices.

Latency teaches us something important about social rejection, discrimination, and racism. *In a group of people based on shared, uniform values and rules, which all members obey out of an internal faith in these values, there can be no racism and discrimination.* Studies in social psychology indicate that discrimination and racism exist between groups. But the most serious discrimination, racism, and rejection will be applied to an individual or sub-group belonging to the group, living within it, but not precisely applying, or opposing, the system of rules and values of the society in which they live. In other words, holding distinguishing values within the belonging group awakens the highest levels of social rejection. The cruelest racism and discrimination will be applied in cases where the child is distinguished by the self core function, which is an unconscious and covert part of the self. Nobody outside can see it clearly, just feel it unconsciously.

Teacher intervention according to the developmental paradigm

First, here are some examples of difficulties in the education system as it is today:

1   A homeroom teacher of the fourth grade describes the class queen as abusing the girls in her class.
2   A homeroom teacher reports that the subject teachers complain about constant interruptions in their lessons.
3   A fifth-grade homeroom teacher complains that children in her class behave cruelly to one boy and that she can't do anything to prevent this.
4   A fourth-grade homeroom teacher complains that the children appeal to her with any social matter, large or small, even after school hours.

These cases indicate the difficulties created in classrooms where the teachers lack developmental understanding of the needs of this age group, the role of teachers, the class hierarchy, social norms, and so on.

Elements of the educational approach according to the developmental paradigm

Class diagnosis

The purpose of diagnosis is to determine the class's maturity level in order to adapt the educational approach to the class's characteristics. The maturity axis extends between two poles: the childhood self and the social self.

The childhood self pole: a state of immaturity, where the children exist in a state of willfulness that doesn't enable them to exist in the function of subordination in the social self. This can be seen in several prominent characteristics:

1   The children are focused on expressing their opinion, realizing their will while seeing exclusively themselves, without any reference to the perspectives of other people. They can say things like, "This is my opinion, and I don't care at all what others think".
2   The children can only exist in situations when they're the center and when they're winning. They find it very difficult to accept situations where others win or are the center of attention.
3   Usually, immature children respond to frustration in infantile ways: crying, physical or verbal violence, informing.

4 The teacher is the main significant figure the children will approach about any social issue, expecting him or her to solve all their problems. The children accept the teacher's authority and behave accordingly. The children also have a strong need for the teacher's attention, appreciation, and admiration.

5 The children often mention their parents as having exclusive authority over their social behavior.

6 The children tend to have interpersonal friendships rather than group friendships.

7 The children don't treat members of the opposite sex with revulsion, quite the opposite, they seek out their company.

8 The children tend to express their personal opinions honestly, directly, and without taking into account social factors that don't enable this and necessitate a diplomatic and sometimes "hypocritical" approach.

The social self pole: a situation of maturity, where the children exist in a state of subordination. This can be seen in several prominent characteristics:

1 The children concentrate on social matters, obey the class rulers, take into consideration the opinion of the popular children, and often speak in terms of "we" and "us".

2 The children behave and act similarly to the popular children in the class.

3 The children know how to accept defeat and not to be the center of attention. In fact, they want to enable the class rulers to win at their expense, and accept their centrality and control willingly and cooperatively.

4 The children observe gender separation.

5 The children express their frustrations verbally.

6 The children accept the authority of their classmates and allow themselves to breach the teacher's authority. They feel that they don't depend on the teacher's appreciation, but seek appreciation from the class through behaviors that the children appreciate. For example, a boy can make the class laugh because he'll receive appreciation and support from the children, even at the cost of a possible reprimand or punishment from the teacher.

7 They behave with social "cruelty" according to the social need.

Teacher intervention based on the diagnosis

According to the developmental paradigm, the teacher is expected to help especially children who are in an immature state – in a childhood self state that doesn't allow them to adapt themselves to the latency developmental stage, where the group of children acts and functions as an independent society, without particular dependence on a significant adult. How should the teacher act in order to help them progress and develop to transition into the next stage, subordination in the social self? The teacher should employ two methods in parallel:

1   Paradoxically, the teacher should spend time with these children in their immature developmental stage. As long as the children are unable to move to the next stage and behave in accordance with the emotional developmental stage previous to their age, the teacher should provide them with these early needs. Among these infantile needs: the need for the teacher's exclusive admiration for the child; allowing the child to act in a way that allows the teacher to appreciate him or her as a good child; allowing him or her to "inform" without criticism; helping the child during difficulties; and being a significant figure in problem solving. The teacher should also continue to provide reinforcement, to facilitate studies, and so on. In this situation, the homeroom teacher should provide these early needs as much as possible. Thus, for example, when an immature child expresses his or her opinion and doesn't pay attention to the rest of the class that doesn't allow an individual to take up so much time in the public space, allow the child to speak and even consider his or her words aloud. When the teacher reprimands the child: "John, you must understand that there are other children here! I can't let just you speak. Be considerate of others", the child isn't receiving satisfaction of these early needs, and this lack of satisfaction causes a developmental delay. In addition, this shines a spotlight on the child's being anomalous in the class.

   The teacher should also enable situations where the delayed children win, and should give all the immature children winners' feedback, even if they're not winners and not successful, and even if their answers are incorrect. Their internal reality, as we've seen, doesn't allow them to accept external criticism. The quality of the self core is controlled by an egocentric, omnipotent, and grandiose internal reality. This quality doesn't enable them to handle situations of failure or loss. Therefore, the teacher should understand that children in the function of willfulness must have these infantile needs satisfied. Thus, where there is competition between children, the immature children must receive praise for their great abilities. They must receive a message of winning, even if this is contrary to reality. Exposing these children to situations of failure or loss should be in accordance with the child's ability to accept and bear this. The teacher should test this ability carefully and gradually expose them to the external reality, in accordance with the children's limitations. Only fulfilling the infantile needs of the self core can lead them to continue developing so that they can transition to the function of subordination, and thus exist in a condition where they no longer have such a strong need to be in the center, omnipotent, and to have exclusive control. The teacher's response to infantile forms of expressing frustration should be understanding and calming. Usually, when elementary schoolchildren cry or react violently, the adults and other children respond aggressively: "Crying like a baby!", "Stop behaving like a baby!", "Grow up!", "Speak! Use words to say what you want so we can understand you!" But big children crying like babies are indeed immature and still in the childhood self, so they must continue, even at their age, to be addressed with an attitude suitable for the earlier stages. This is the same compassionate and understanding attitude employed with younger children: "I understand, John, that you've been very hurt, that you're crying with pain and sorrow". Only an understanding and considerate approach, containing their hurt, can provide a soft, empathic response to the early unsatisfied needs, and over time, enable the children to transition to the social self. While this might sound strange and counterintuitive, mature children during latency don't need this attitude.

2   In addition to the help the teacher should provide to the immature children who are still in the function of willfulness, finding solutions to problems and solving social conflicts, he or she should also protect them from harm by other children in the class, who are unwilling to accept egocentric or controlling behaviors and might harm these children with social rejection. For this purpose, the homeroom teacher must inform the immature children of the advantages of adapting themselves to the norms and rules that are accepted in the class. For this purpose, the teacher should use the principles of individual therapy, the Envelopes Therapy method.

Using the principles of individual therapy – Envelopes Therapy – for class intervention

Children are frequently socially rejected. The meaning of their rejection is that they are acting immaturely, in the function of the childhood self, and not transitioning to the social self. Social rejection and other things like social arguments and class disputes result from this reason. The teacher's aim is to help the immature children adapt themselves to the social self function, in which the other children in the class, or most of them, exist. This is done in accordance with the principles of individual therapy. This means that in any matter, an argument during class, a game during recess, shared activity where conflicts arise between the individual's will and the group's will, the teacher must help the immature children subordinate themselves to the social norms. This is achieved using the principles of individual therapy presented in the previous chapter. First, in cases of social difficulties, the teacher presents to the children the two directions: 1. my personal will; 2. the group's will, and describes the meaning of these two directions: 1. willfulness; 2. subordination, emphasizing two important issues in the context of these two conditions:

1   The choice is theirs. They decide which way to choose. Control is in their own hands.

2   Each choice has advantages and disadvantages. The advantage in choosing the first direction of personal will and willfulness is that it gives a wonderful feeling of not surrendering one's personal will. The price of choosing this direction is social rejection. The advantage of the second direction, of the group's will, is that it leads to social belonging and acceptance, and thus children feel good about themselves. They are not stressed and suffering. Their self-esteem is high, and they continue developing. The cost of this choice is the unbearable and almost impossible pain and difficulty of surrendering one's personal will.

Social rejection during latency will be reduced significantly when the teachers act according to the principles described, based on the developmental paradigm.

How can the teacher identify the moment when his or her role in helping an immature child ends, and now he or she should allow the child to move on to the next developmental stage, establishing the development of the social self in the class by participating in its independent activity and reducing dependence on the teacher? Precisely when the teacher feels that the child is no longer paying so much attention to him or her, this is the wonderful sign of progress in development. When the teacher feels that the child has received sufficient nourishing, so he or she is saturated with infantile treatment, when the child approaches the other children and pays less attention to the teacher, then the teacher knows that his or her role in facilitating the child's transition to the next developmental stage has come to an end.

In other words, the teacher should treat immature children who are still in the function of willfulness the same way and with the same quality that was provided when they were in kindergarten or first grade: a soft, compassionate attitude to an infant. Teachers who do this describe a strange feeling at first for giving an infantile, even sometimes "babyish", treatment to an older child in class. However, this is the correct way for developmental growth. Also, the teacher should work in collaboration with the parents. Since the immature child is in a state of childhood self, the parents are still very dominant. They have to receive the same messages given to the teacher, and they too should provide the child's grandiose, omnipotent, and exclusive control needs. In parallel, the parents should support the teacher's move of protecting the child in the latency social reality and to support the choice options presented to the child by the teacher.

Reducing the teacher's authority and intervention

In contrast with the early years of school, when the teacher was a significant figure for the children, in third to fifth grade, the society of the class children becomes the most significant selfobject. The teacher's place is preserved as a significant and important figure, but the children seek to form an independent society in which adults have less and less of a foothold. The teacher, like parental figures and adults in general, is perceived as remote from the children's social world experience. The rules and the dynamics within the group of children are far removed from the teacher's eyes and are no longer subject to supervision. This is a world whose rules establish the society of children. These are strong rules, including arbitrary social norms that don't accord with the canonical moral rules of the general society.

Strong teachers who employ their authority to impose their canonical rules will disrupt the important developmental process of forming independent social norms and rules, delay the development, or, alternatively, the class, if sufficiently strong, will continue to develop far from the teachers' eyes or else revolt and breach the teachers' authority openly and flagrantly.

Weak, unauthoritative teachers, whose presence is irrelevant in the children's eyes, or who fight, insult, and threaten them, sometimes offending their dignity, also fail to enable the continued proper social development. Such behavior not only disrupts continued development, but even harms the children's emotional development. For example: Rachel, who wished to establish her social status by being impertinent to the teacher and threatening his authority, would be severely harmed if the teacher whose authority was violated retaliated by insulting her in front of the whole class. The teacher's response to the student has to take this developmental component into account. On the one hand, the teacher must establish a clear boundary by not accepting disrespect, but on the other hand, the teacher must understand the student's behavior from a developmental aspect. Thus, for example an appropriate response from the teacher could be: "I understand that you don't accept what I'm saying and I see that other children in the class agree with you. I respect this. In the same way, you should speak to me politely and respectfully".

Children at this age greatly need teachers with an accepting, authoritative attitude who don't enforce their values in a controlling manner. These are teachers who enable the existence of an appropriate cultivation space for the children's developmental needs: allowing the society of class children to express opinions opposed to their own and to behave according to norms that differ from the moral rules accepted by the general society. Such teachers respect the existence of an independent society of class children, with its own hierarchy and norms. They also appreciate the efforts of each child to gain a place within this society by joining the general social force and acting accordingly.

The children perceive the teacher's reactions and are sometimes influenced by them, and this can impact a child's place and status in the class. For example, a correct response to John, who tells a joke in the middle of the lesson and gets all the class laughing, is "Well done! That was funny, and you made all the children laugh. Now, let's hear how you handle the next topic in this lesson". In this way, the lesson can continue. This is a developmentally correct response. The teacher's main role is to help the children establish their society as an independent society, to be a protective, understanding, and accepting figure, thus helping them to determine how their society works, define the extent of its authority, and understand and see the rules and norms it creates by itself.

The teacher should help the children transition from the stage of exclusive dependence on him or her to the stage where they are an independent society of children. This developmental transition to social independence is not simple. While the children feel that the society of children gives them the power to make this transition, they still require adult support to enable this, to calm things down, to see this development in a positive, supporting light, rather than as we tend to think today, when we fight them and consider them bad and cruel children who are impertinent and lack conscience. Thus, for instance, when the children ask for the teacher's intervention in social disputes within the class, the teacher should express sorrow about the situation that has occurred, the hurt, anger, and insult that the children are experiencing, and at the same time he or she should express confidence in their ability to solve this dispute by themselves. When a group of girls comes back from recess complaining about each other, the teacher should reflect and express identification: "It's not pleasant to fight", and at the same time encourage them to deal with it independently: "But I trust you to find the right way to solve this problem yourselves".

Often, developmentally delayed children ask the homeroom teacher for help with social issues. They don't understand why the teacher doesn't intervene and allows the children who control the class to behave arbitrarily, sometimes "cruelly", unfairly, and inconsistently. They feel disappointed by their teacher and feel that he or she is failing by not intervening and changing the class dynamics, where one group of students is higher in the hierarchy above the others, establishes social norms that aren't moral or acceptable, and the rest of the class obeys them and even strengthens the power of this unjust dynamic. Children who are still immature and exist in their childhood self are in great distress. They experience injustice regarding the class hierarchy and immoral norms, and also feel it's unjust that the teacher isn't acting according to the childhood self, where he or she is the most significant figure who decides everything, has authority and power, and should use rewards and punishments to determine who's a good child. Instead, the teacher leaves the society of children to exist "lawlessly". Immature children watch the teacher's helplessness to impose his or her power and authority to restore what they see as the right justice. They find it hard to accept this and interpret the teacher's avoiding intervening as injustice that is added to the social injustice of the children. These children will continue appealing to the teacher to intervene in social issues. This happens mainly at the end of recess, when the children return to the class, and the lesson can't start because they are brimming with complaints: "Teacher, look what he did to me . . .". At present, teachers tend to approach these complaints with conflict resolution tools. They try to "mediate" between the two parties, find out the motive of each side, and punish whomever they find responsible. The correct approach, according to the developmental paradigm presented here, is to clarify what the group wants in the dispute, and what the individual wants. Children should be helped to transition to subordination to the group's will. If a child finds this transition difficult, he or she should be invited to an individual meeting, given warm, personal treatment supporting the selfobject appropriate to younger ages: unique admiration, omnipotence, and control. However, he or she should be presented with the choice described above, in the Envelopes Therapy.

The teacher's role

Now let's present the teacher's role in different situations.

The teacher's role regarding individual children

During latency, the teacher's role is to help children develop and transition from a state of willfulness to a state of subordination. For this purpose, the teacher has to move along an axis with two poles. At one pole are the immature children. For such children, the teacher is the most significant figure. These children expect the teacher to provide them with individual attention, impose law and order, give them rewards and punishments according to their behavior, and be impressed by their good behavior. At the other pole, the teacher is a significant figure who supports the children's ability to maintain an independent society in which children determine the group's identity and operate in accordance with the group's hierarchy and norms. The teacher's role here is as an enabling presence that supports the group's operation.

The teacher's role with immature children: immature children can't manage without the teacher. They need him or her very much. They turn to him or her in all matters, expect attention and admiration, and obey his or her instructions and education. Therefore, the teacher's preliminary position is to adapt to these children's developmental stage, to form a personal connection with them, to provide positive rewards for their good behavior, to legitimize their personal will and good morality. From this starting point, the teacher should gradually help the children transition to the social self by directing the spotlight to the correct choice. He or she should illuminate the advantages of adapting to the group, and address them less often so they try to get along by themselves, according to the children's group's desired norms.

The teacher's role with mature children existing in the "subordination" function: most of the children in fourth and fifth grade exist in this function; they are mature children. They require the independent management of their society, without adult intervention. The teacher's role with the mature children is to enable them to do this, not to create a personal connection with them, and not to enforce authority and control. The mature children don't need personal attention or admiration from their teacher. Nor do they need the teacher's authority, instruction, or education. Often at this stage of children's development the parents and teachers experience difficulty due to being pushed aside again and again. At each developmental stage, the role of parents and significant adults is to enable the children freedom to develop separate independence. Despite all the difficulty, it's important to remember that this is the natural, desirable developmental process. At each stage, children acquire more and more independent abilities, and the caring figure must permit this. Many good parents and teachers have trouble accepting this and remain dominant in the children's lives. During latency, good teachers are those who relinquish their authority and control to the society of children. They do this because they understand that the children are not fighting or disrespecting their authority. The children do this when the significant adults don't understand that they must move aside. Each year that passes, from third grade onward, children require more independence for their group. In the fifth grade, the children already wish to manage the social life of their class by themselves.

The teachers' role is to help them strengthen their group identity rather than try to dictate to them social activities for social cohesion. They shouldn't intervene in the social hierarchy or fight the class rulers or the norms they create. Nor should they appeal to the parents for help in certain social situations. The parents of the strong children shouldn't be asked to moderate their children, either. This is because just as the children no longer involve their teachers in their social life, they also involve their parents less and less. Asking the parents to intervene harms the children's development. Teachers should act in the opposite direction, helping the children reject the parents' attempt to intervene in their affairs. They should explain to the parents the importance of the children managing their society independently without interference.

The teacher's role in cases of social rejection: I shall demonstrate the teacher's role in cases of social rejection with an example. The parents of a second-grade girl come to a meeting with the school staff. In cracking voices, they describe the terrible situation of their daughter, a gifted, attractive, gentle, good child. The parents describe her developmental background, noting that in the first grade, her situation had been excellent. The girl easily mastered reading and writing, and was popular with children in her class. In contrast, this year she seems "switched off". She comes back from school saying that all the girls chase her away. She's also dropping in her studies. She's completely stopped taking any interest in the activities she previously did with her parents. They say that the girl describes a social situation where there are popular and less popular girls, and she's the least popular. The girls insult her, call her names, and humiliate her. She asks them to buy her clothes and shoes from a certain brand, like those the popular girls have, but the parents refuse due to their principles and values of modesty. They claim that she manipulates them to buy these clothes, and they keep refusing. Following their refusal, their daughter demonstrates these parental values among her classmates. When they talk about expensive clothes, she tells them that what's important is internal values rather than external appearance. In response, the girls reject her from their company, and she remains alone and isolated. As a result, she experiences anxiety and low self-confidence. She feels ugly and unattractive, and says that nobody in her class likes her. Even her best friend from kindergarten abandoned her for other, popular friends, and the parents are very angry that this friend is "cheating" on their daughter. With further questioning, the parents report that they invite girls over in the afternoon and see that their daughter has excellent relations with them. When the connection is one on one, it's easy for her. The difficulty is in group friendships. She isn't invited back to their homes, and at school these girls ignore her.

The parents blame the school staff for not doing enough to improve their daughter's social situation. They complain that the teachers don't know what goes on outside during recess, when she's alone, and that they don't stand beside her when she's being hurt. Her homeroom teacher becomes defensive, and tells the parents that in the class she can't see that their daughter is lonely at all.

Let's examine this case according to the age's developmental needs:

1 The girl wants to be similar to the other girls, by wearing brands, but the parents refuse.
2 The parents encourage her to stick to the household's modesty norms.
3 The parents invite "good friends" to their home and are upset when her best friend from kindergarten leaves her for other friends.
4 The girl suffers from social rejection due to not accepting the social norms and sticking to her parents' values.
5 Social rejection damages the girl's self-image and self-esteem, and she feels ugly and unloved.

Conclusion: The parents aren't helping their daughter make the transition to the social self. They should help her buy the class's popular brands and not insist on the household values, but help the girl adapt herself to the class's values. Also, the parents shouldn't encourage interpersonal friendships with best friends. Nor should they be angry at the "best friend" from kindergarten who left their daughter in favor of other friends. They should understand that this is an essential developmental move, and as we have seen earlier, this is precisely the appropriate type of friendship for latency.

The teacher's role is to act on two levels. On the most essential level, the teacher and the school's psychological staff should give the parents the developmental explanation and help them release their daughter to social behavior within the class. On the second level, the teacher should let the girl know that her desire to behave according to the class norms is important and positive, and should encourage this behavior.

The teacher's role in strengthening the hierarchy: when children are asked who a class queen or class king is, they will usually answer that this is someone with lots of power, who chooses his or her close friends, someone everyone wants to be friends with, who controls everyone, tells them what to do, and that everyone has to give in to. Children tend to believe that the class rulers decide about rejecting a child, ostracism, and they also determine the clothing style, speech style, class atmosphere, and behavioral norms. Children who aren't allowed to curse at home start cursing under instruction from the class king or queen; girls want to style their hair according to the class queen's fashion. Children report that the class rulers are the most successful, most loved, strongest, most popular, best at sport, most attractive, most amazing, and that all the children in class admire them. Like the children, the students' parents are drawn into this empowering view. Parents of children whom the class rulers dislike develop hostility toward the class rulers of their children's class. Sometimes, parents in distress feel the need to fight the class rulers physically, to repay them for their treatment of their child. In many parents' view, the class rulers possess too much power. The teachers also fall into the same glorifying trap, and often see the power and authority of the class rulers as a threat to be fought. Because the class rulers dictate behavioral norms that often contradict the school's morality (violence, humiliation, cursing, etc.), the teachers employ their authority and power against the creators of these norms, sometimes trying to break the resolve of the class rulers and their popular supporters. But the class rulers serve an essential role from a developmental point of view. First, they fulfill a role in the children's need to belong to a body that is elevated and more powerful than them. Like an Oedipal father at an earlier age, the society of children serves the same need for idealism. The class rulers also play an important role in establishing the class norms that strengthen the class hierarchy, which enables a feedback circle creating the uniformity and twinship that are so important developmentally. The class rulers also dictate behavioral norms that differ from those of the home or the school, and thus force the children to free themselves from their childhood chains and adapt themselves to the next stage, where the society of children is independent and functions without the presence of adults in setting and enforcing norms.

The teacher has an important role in granting appropriate developmental space for the existence of the class rulers. We could even say that the existence of class rulers is critically important for the psychic development of the class's children. The structure of the class nest depends upon them. So, it's important to maintain their existence and treat their status carefully.

From a psychic point of view, the class rulers exist in an opposite emotional state to what the children, parents, and teachers perceive. Their psychic state is fragile. First, they are no less anxious than others regarding their status, and every day they fight to maintain their social status, usually investing time, thought, and energy in this. Adults who were class rulers during childhood often describe it as follows: "I was constantly worried that I'd be brought down"; "Some children hated me because I was class king"; "I was attacked"; "They fought me!". One of the explanations for their strong need to be in the center of social life stems precisely from an early unsatisfied developmental need. Often, the class rulers need the children's love and admiration really desperately. Sometimes the class rulers demand from the class a response to a need from earlier stages in their lives, when they suffered from deficits. For example, a class queen used to tell all the girls that her dad was a magician and could do magic, and all the girls had to nod and affirm her story. They didn't really believe her but gave her the feeling that she was telling the truth. Another class queen boasted that her parents were friends with celebrities, and another forced the girls to give her valuable gifts they had received from their parents, which she didn't have. Such expressions are the outcome of unsatisfied needs. The class rulers' central position in the class is thus a lifebelt for them. They need this central place like air. It enables them to insist upon their demands and find themselves a constant source of satisfaction for those needs.

Sometimes there are classes where several children aim to be class rulers. These are all children who are still in the willfulness function of the childhood self, who need the continued satisfaction of their early developmental need. They are all in the early position of wanting to be in the center, controlling, and grandiose. A struggle develops between several children for the position of ruler. The children who lose to the class rulers often feel very frustrated, because they too have immense needs within the willfulness function, to be in the center, to control, and so on, which go unsatisfied. In fact, the class king or queen has the strongest need and absolutely cannot surrender this position, and often the children who are defeated by the class ruler suffer from social rejection because they can't subordinate themselves and allow someone else to be in the center. Sometimes, when you talk to a class king or queen, you can sense their vulnerability, their sensitivity, their need for a warm, sympathetic, and appreciative attitude.

The teacher should treat the class rulers in two ways:

1 Understand the importance of the existence of class rulers for the existence of the social life typical of this age, the hierarchy and class norms, and acknowledge that this enables a natural and normal growth environment for all the children in the class. Therefore, their authority and control shouldn't be challenged but permitted.

2 Understand the fragile emotional state of the class rulers, and help them gradually transition from a position of childhood self to the social self. First, teachers should adapt their approach to the class rulers' emotional state and need to be at the center. Talk to them warmly and sensitively, encourage them, and treat them well, even giving them appreciating and admiring feedback. Also, allow them to express their wishes, give them positive rewards for being who they are, view them sympathetically and compassionately, and thus help them gradually escape from the demanding role they are fulfilling and continue to develop along with the rest of the class. This gradually allows the class rulers to be rescued from their willfulness position while continuing to maintain their role in the hierarchy until the end of latency.

The teacher's role in changing class norms: the greatest difficulty of teachers and parents is to accept the fact that the society of children in class establishes negative norms, such as violence, ridicule, or humiliation. The path to change these norms is blocked to teachers and parents, as mentioned earlier. So, how can class norms be changed?

The answer is that the adults can't do this, and furthermore, shouldn't do this. As we have seen, there is a clear distinction between class norms and social sanctions. I have worked with dozens of classes, and none of them had particularly explicitly "negative" or hurtful class norms. The norms were usually related to games, clothing, and speech. Sometimes, the norms could include behaviors related to stereotypes: boys showing strength and power; girls interested in conversation and economic status, and so on. These norms are not really harmful, because they are part of the developmental needs. During latency, social behaviors and social norms are not as dangerous as they can be during adolescence: drugs, crime, sex, and so on. During latency the norms have a very low danger level.

The serious violence, humiliation, and oppression that are hurtful during latency are not related to norms but to the social sanctions applied to those who are inaccurate in obeying the norms and not adapted to society in the function of the social self. The cruel behaviors of latency age children are not social norms, but the sanction they impose on those who don't subordinate themselves to the accepted social norms. Thus, teachers shouldn't try to change social norms, but to perceive which of the children are not adapting themselves to the social norms and help them to adapt, thus preventing the cruel and violent sanction of social rejection from being employed. Helping children conform to the norms doesn't necessitate the teacher's finding out the essence and meaning of the social norms. As we have noted, these norms are subtle, rapidly changing, and only the children themselves, being part of the society, can perceive these subtleties. The teachers should help the children focus on perceiving the norms, and they will themselves naturally locate the norms and adapt themselves to them.

The teacher's role regarding social sanctions: as stated earlier, social sanctions play an important role in children's development. I shall present the homeroom teacher's role through a case study:

The parents of some fifth-grade girls ask for an urgent meeting with the school's staff. Most of the class's girls are suffering from a closed group of girls who are abusing the other girls, especially one of them, who is really rejected. The parents describe situations where the girls treat each other really cruelly. This is often not overt, but the class atmosphere is one of intrigues and plots. The homeroom teacher and most of the class's girls describe the strong girls as imposing an atmosphere of fear and terror. The girls can't concentrate on their studies and live in constant fear. Whoever does something the strong girls don't like is subjected to gossip and libel. There is often gossip, even within the group of strong girls. The wicked gossip causes the girls to remain silent and afraid. The class queen is described as the most harmful of all. She appears externally as "the best girl in the world", but she's described by the teacher and most of the girls as a "really bad girl". The parents describe the strong girls in the class as "bad girls" who can't be trusted.

Due to the severe class atmosphere, most of the girls prefer not to participate in social activities. The teacher, an impressive personality admired by the rest of the school's staff, who took it upon herself to handle this challenging class, made great efforts to change the social situation in the class. She connected with the girls, shared their secrets, followed their norms, and thus created a relationship of trust with them. But after a while, the girls treated her as one of them, and on one occasion treated her the way they treat each other. They gossiped about the teacher and told their parents that the teacher gossips about some of the girls. The parents threatened the teacher and principal, claiming that the girls reported that the teacher gossips about some of the girls. The devoted teacher, who had acted fairly and faithfully with a strong internal motivation to improve the social situation, was astonished and hurt by the girls' cruelty. She hadn't understood the severity of the popular girls' hurting other girls until they hurt her the same way and she could feel how harmful it was. The personal hurting of the teacher changed her attitude to the girls entirely. Now, being hurt, she remembered all their cruel actions, especially those of the class queen. She gave an example of a case where one of the girls had lost her father. In order to help the children handle this situation, the teacher and school staff gathered the class and spoke to them about their feelings regarding the death of one of the girls' father. When leaving the lesson, one of the girls started crying, identifying with the bereaved girl. The "wicked" class queen went up to her angrily and said: "Why are you crying? Is it your dad?"

The parents were furious and expressed a firm position to the teacher. They were unwilling to accept the teacher's position and accused her of not behaving like an educator.

An analysis of the case indicates a group of girls most of whom are in the immature state of the childhood self. The "bad" group of popular girls "works" hard, because the other girls don't accept the hierarchy and don't obey their norms. Also, most of the girls have opinionated parents (who are also in a state of willfulness) who interfere in their daughters' lives and contribute to their developmental delay. The severe sanctions of the popular girls are unable to change the condition of the delayed girls. Even the sanction they imposed on the teacher didn't contribute to their efforts. This class has a group of mature girls who are working to lead the class nest into the function of subordination. The immature girls, supported by their parents, are fighting them and frustrating the mature girls' trend. This class is experiencing a severe developmental delay, lacking the power to initiate the transition to the social self.

The options available to the teacher here are:

1 Involve the professionals and discuss each of the girls, examining the causes of immaturity. Perhaps some of the girls have such a large deficit in the early developmental stages that they require psychological therapy.
2 A lecture to the parents on development and recommendations on how to treat the girls' social problems: not to intervene; to encourage them to become similar to the popular girls; to accept the class norms; to accept the hierarchy of popular girls; and to reduce their own power and authority at home to impose their moral values.
3 Strengthen the hierarchy by providing respect to the class queen along with providing the satisfaction of infantile needs (grandiosity, omnipotence, control) to the immature girls.
4 From this dual position, lead the immature girls gradually to accept the popular girls' norms.
5 Since this is not a case of an individual girl or a few girls but the majority of the girls being in the childhood self, the teacher should receive help from professionals and conduct a series of social activities in the class.

References

Fisher-Grafy, H. (2015). *Socially Rejected Children*. Tel Aviv: Resling [Hebrew].
Freedman, S. (1996). Role of selfobject experiences in affective development during latency. *Psychoanalytic Psychology*, 13(1): 101–127.
Winnicott, D.W. (1962). Theory of the parent-infant relationship: Contributions to the discussion. *International Journal of Psychoanalysis*, 43: 256–257.

6   Happy schoolchildren

On the basis of the psychological-developmental paradigm presented in this book, it appears that elementary schools should be designed and structured in a completely different way than they are at present. This chapter will present a new educational approach, which may perhaps even be considered "revolutionary", relying on this book's developmental paradigm.

Many studies have indicated the influence of the social field on all the developmental aspects: student academic achievement, self-esteem, and behavioral control (Eccles et al., 1999; Parker et al., 1995). But the social approach is not sufficient. The influence of the social realm has to be understood through a developmental perspective. The developmental understanding is very important for constructing an age-appropriate educational setting.

Let's demonstrate this with an example for a different developmental stage. When a 2-year-old boy says in an age-appropriate manner that the swing in the public park is "my swing", his perception won't change if we educate him according to objective reality that this swing doesn't belong only to him and that it's public property. This education makes the child's development more difficult, because in his developmental stage, the swing is indeed his. A message that contradicts his internal perception could sabotage his natural development.

Similarly, an educational approach to latency age children should be adapted to their developmental stage. Unfortunately, a hundred years of psychoanalysis have underestimated the importance of development during latency and have failed to provide a unique developmental theory or paradigm for this stage. It appears that the education methods of the last century have been developed without a psychological basis suitable to the age group's developmental needs. Experienced educators feel this lack when every year social problems arise in the third to sixth grades, and particularly in the fourth to fifth grades, and disrupt the school routine. These problems include social violence: disputes and arguments, physical violence, verbal violence, online bullying, humiliation, ostracism, rebelling against the teachers' authority, disrupting the school's routine and rules. The lack of developmental knowledge is what causes the problems in classes. It's not the teachers and education system who should be blamed for this, but the absence of developmental understanding of this stage.

Educational approach adapted to the latency developmental stage

I propose that the purpose of school, according to this book's developmental approach, is to serve as a developmental hothouse for the age's needs. This means enabling the children to establish an independent society with its own hierarchy and social norms. This is somewhat reminiscent of Jean Jacques Rousseau's position whereby children at this stage should be free of external supervision. He considered formal education as harmful and suggested postponing it to the start of adolescence (Rousseau, 1921). The educational approach presented here is to allow the independent group of children to be free of dependence on the framework imposed by adults, to allow a developmental hothouse where each child's intrapsychic development occurs individually within the framework of the classmates' group. The emphasis in this approach is on the social framework of classmates. This is where the developmental transition occurs from the childhood self to the social self. The school as a hothouse will suit this purpose when it allows the children to operate according to the social self, where the children become subordinate and accept the social norms, obey those higher than them in the hierarchy, and become sensitive and receptive to social changes, with an independent social existence that doesn't rely on significant adults. The school's role, together with the parents, is to enable this development while strengthening and supporting the developmental process. The appropriate support is expressed in reducing the intervention of parents and teachers and providing sensitive and containing support for the hierarchy and social norms. The homeroom teacher's main role can be, metaphorically, to return the chicks that escape from the flock back into the fold and help them move in the same direction as the flock. At this age, children repeatedly slip up and engage in an individualistic escape in the direction of personal will and the inability to move flexibly in the direction of the group's movement.

The teacher should ensure that the anomalous children return to the group. All children, including the class rulers, sometimes encounter situations where they make a personal choice rather than a group choice. All children, regardless of their abilities and maturity, sometimes experience situations where they find it hard to follow the group. In adulthood, too, we encounter cases where the majority decides something and the individual finds it difficult to accept the majority's decision. Individuals reject the majority decision just because it differs from their own preference. Latency is the age when this function develops and children acquire the adaptive ability to adjust themselves to society, even when this sometimes clashes with their own personal will. As mentioned earlier, this function is no less important than the function of psychic willfulness. Thus, the teacher's role is to serve as a shepherd observing and supervising when one of the flock deviates from the general direction. The rapid shifts in the children's direction and the frequent changes in the social norms, which are unclear to adults, are very important in developing the children's psychic flexibility. Teachers play an important and significant role in maintaining the safe existence of the whole group of children functioning autonomously.

The assumption today is that it's impossible to grant responsibility and authority to the group of children and that it's absolutely impossible to surrender the centralist authority and status of teachers in all areas of the children's lives at school. This approach stems from the low awareness of the children's developing abilities and from the adults' psychological difficulty in surrendering their central role in the children's lives. According to the developmental paradigm presented here, the society of children should be allowed to exist in a manner appropriate to the developmental stage and to construct their social basis independently, with a minimum level of external adult intervention. The presence of adults is essential, but their role is to facilitate the independent existence of the children's group. Each adult intervention in the society of children's independent construct violates the sanctity of this natural development. For example: if teachers participate in determining the class social hierarchy, they remain significant adult figures who remove control from the children. Even if the teachers get the impression that the children accept the hierarchy they suggested, under the surface the children will reject it and maintain their own hierarchy.

The teachers' presence is essential in helping the group of children exist without them. Their role is to transfer the arena of class occurrences in all areas, including learning, to the social arena. Children at this age develop, study, and function when they are in the developmental environment appropriate to the latency stage: an independent and autonomous society. Moreover, the development of the individual child's psyche in the social self cytoplasm and in the subordination function occurs in the developmental substrate of the autonomous class.

Gradual program for transferring authority to the society of children

First, we should note that latency age children are interested in the group dynamic of their own gender, and the social life of the other gender doesn't interest them. We could exaggerate and say that lessons that discuss the social lives of the boys don't interest the girls, and vice versa. During latency, the structure of studies should be adapted so that each of the genders is focused on its natural social belonging. Each of the genders has a different stereotype and different behavioral expectations, and the mode of social belonging differs between the genders. Often children return from recess complaining about arguments and disputes: the boys often discuss problems that happened on the sporting field, while the girls are engaged with difficulties in the relations between them, operating in small groups.

Guiding principle

The program's guiding principle is: the children determine their behavior in the school. This doesn't refer only to studying but to all areas of life in the classroom. The teacher's intervention in the children's decisions is gradually reduced from the first grade to the sixth grade. There is a solid basis of research supporting the developmental fact that teachers' authority is reduced in elementary school (Laupa, 1991; Laupa & Turiel, 1986), and that acceptance of educational authority is influenced by social factors (Laupa & Turiel, 1993).

The social language should be established already from the first grade. The homeroom teacher gives roles and tasks to the entire class, teaches the behavioral roles in the group, which is the whole class, and the appropriate means of communication. In the first grade, when the transition from the childhood self occurs, the teacher is still the primary person who determines behavior. In the second grade, the teacher includes the children's opinion in determining behavior. Each year, the authority of the society of children increases, with the teacher enabling this authority to exist and accordingly relinquishing authority to the society of children. In the third grade, the teacher and the society of children determine behavior through dialogue between them. In the fourth grade, the children determine behavior, with the teacher helping when required in situations where the children's decision-making process encounters difficulties. In the fifth grade, the children are already skilled and know how to establish their own procedures, and the teacher is more of an observer, while assisting individuals who deviate from the group's direction. In the sixth grade, the children determine behavior, but gradually, according to the transition to the next stage, adolescence, the teacher returns to being a central and significant figure in addition to the society of children.

The school's purpose according to the developmental approach is to constitute a developmental growing space for children in the process of shaping them as mature, moral people who fulfill their internal destiny in their society. Educating for the generic values is not appropriate for the latency developmental stage. This value education is appropriate for infancy and ends in the first or second grade, and is then resumed towards adolescence, in the sixth grade. During latency, as has been found in the studies mentioned earlier, the children obey their independent social norms rather than the generic morality. Also, studying and acquiring knowledge detached from the social fabric is unsuitable to this age. The current perception is that the supreme aim of school is to lead students to acquire knowledge and education for moral values, with the main purpose of time spent at school being academic and professional lessons, with short breaks or recesses for letting off steam. However, the perception here is that the central occurrence at school is social, and requires time, and so it occurs primarily during activities such as the current recesses and classes with a social format. The breaks should be placed as a top priority of the education system, and the primary understanding and energies of the educators should be devoted to them. In fact, the idea is to conduct the breaks as they are today as the central space for the class's existence, which includes studying among other things, with the society of children guiding the contents and methods of learning. The approach presented here suggests that when the children's time spent at school is appropriate to their developmental needs, there will be no need to distinguish between breaks and lessons. The children will feel pleasure and developmental joy at every moment in school.

Breaks: social activity

The breaks, according to the current curriculum, are short periods of fresh air between the lessons enforced on the children. Usually, the children go out of the school building to an open yard where they can vent their energy and are free in their social world. This is a world without the rules and order of the adult world, without any adults present to help the children establish their realm as a beneficial, supportive, and containing realm. The children themselves often create a realm with strict, unsafe rules that awaken anxiety and discomfort.

The social curriculum proposed here includes a break composed of three parts lasting 30 minutes each during the school day, a total of one and a half hours. In the first part, the society of children discusses and determines the planned class activity. The children determine the order and contents. In the second part, the children conduct the activity themselves, with minimal intervention by the teacher. In the third part, the class conducts a discussion of the children's experiences during the activity. At this stage, the teacher should only intervene in order to strengthen the group's independence. The teacher shouldn't impose his or her values and conclusions, but should direct the spotlight to the group and illuminate the power and ability of the society of children to interpret and draw conclusions regarding what occurred during the activity. In the lower grades, the homeroom teacher can suggest a range of game options. For the boys: sporting games, social ball games, card games, and social games like catch or hide-and-seek, collections, building, arts and crafts, power games, and so on. For the girls: sporting games like jumping rope, group discussions of family and social issues, arts and crafts, dancing, and so on. The group of children decides how each game or activity is conducted. The teacher's role over the years is to shape the society of children's ability to discuss the details of the chosen activity. For example, if the group of girls chooses a dancing activity, the teacher can help them shape their choice: type of dance, style (free dancing or learning moves), who teaches the moves? Who's the girls' representative? What's the decision-making process? In the third part, after the dancing activity, group conversations discuss personal experiences during the activity. The teacher's role in this part is to focus on helping the immature children who aren't able to integrate socially during the discussed activity. First, the teacher should protect them from being hurt during the activity, and second, he or she should speak with the children individually and help them on the basis of the Envelopes Therapy principles and increase their "sensors" to become receptive to the class norms.

In the early years, the teacher is actively involved. In the first and second grade, the teacher is dominant in choices and decisions regarding the break activities and also handles the social difficulties that arise, along with explaining the importance of discipline and participation in the activity chosen by the majority of the class's children, and encouraging the adaptation of individual will to the majority's wishes. In the higher classes, the teacher's dominance is reduced and the children manage the activity themselves. As the children grow and the teacher's intervention decreases, we can expect the mature children to accept a decision instantly. The immature children will tend to argue with the rest of their classmates. The teacher's role is to help those who find it difficult to subordinate themselves socially and help accept the norms and social hierarchy.

Collaborative learning

It has been found that children learning in pairs or small groups is preferable to individual learning and advances the children in all areas (Rohrbeck et al., 2003). According to the approach presented here, collaborative learning includes the whole class and is mostly determined by the society of class children. The children determine the studied contents, the learning method, and the process.

Models dictated by educators actually harm the developmental process. Learning strategies that suit adults don't suit latency stage children. The children develop unique social strategies for the developmental stage by themselves. Sometimes it appears to the adults that their way is disorganized, impulsive, and superficial, but this way is the most appropriate for their specific developmental stage.

There is no reason to fear that the children will wander, lose their way, give up, or stop learning and investigating. Social learning itself stems naturally from the developmental needs. However, the teacher can remain dominant in the classroom, keeping in the back of his or her mind the awareness and understanding of the developmental need for an independent society of children in the class. It's important to stress that the educator's role in the learning process is as a quiet, beneficial presence helping the children to function by themselves and assisting those who deviate from the group.

Children with special needs

Children with special needs can be integrated into a school based on the developmental approach. A study on social rejection found that children prefer to accept those with lower academic achievements rather than children who harm the group (Gasser et al., 2017). As we saw earlier, even different and diverse children can belong to the society of classmates when they accept the hierarchy and social norms and exist in a state of twinship with the children in the class. Thus, children with special needs can become an integral part of the regular class when they are integrated without grades and evaluations that sabotage their self-esteem and self-image. The society of children respects each individual who follows the group's social rules. Anyone who does this is accepted and they don't see an innate or acquired disability or difficulty as something that should restrict the child's social integration.

The society of children naturally knows how to behave with children with disabilities and difficulties and to lead them, together with the entire group, to the aims it chooses. According to the paradigm presented here, children with educational difficulties and learning disabilities can integrate into the society of classmates when they behave socially according to the class's accepted social codes. Children with special needs who behave uniformly and belong to the class through "group twinship" can expect to integrate well into the society of children. The social framework supports them so they don't have to experience the shame, lack of self-value, and inferiority that the education system causes them when it primarily values the individual achievements of each student, gives grades and reports, and inflicts developmental injustice upon children in general and particularly those with special needs.

References

Eccles, J.S., Roeser, R., Wigfield, A., & Freedman-Doan, C. (1999). Academic and motivational pathways through middle childhood. In *Child Psychology: A Handbook of Contemporary Issues*, edited by L. Balter & C.S. Tamis-LeMonda (pp. 287–317). Philadelphia: Psychology Press/Taylor & Francis.

Gasser, L., Grütter, J., Torchetti, L., & Buholzer, A. (2017). Competitive classroom norms and exclusion of children with academic and behavior difficulties. *Journal of Applied Developmental Psychology*, 49: 1–11.

Laupa, M. (1991). Children's reasoning about three authority attributes: Adults status, knowledge, and social position. *Developmental Psychology*, 27: 321–329.

Laupa, M. & Turiel, E. (1986). Children's conceptions of adult and peer authority. *Child Development*, 57: 405–412.

Laupa, M. & Turiel, E. (1993). Children's concepts of authority and social contexts. *Journal of Educational Psychology*, 85(1): 191–197.

Parker, J.G., Rubin, K.H., Price, J.M., & DeRosier, M.E. (1995). Peer relationships, child development, and adjustment: A developmental psychopathology perspective. In *Developmental Psychopathology, Vol. 2: Risk, Disorder, and Adaptation*, edited by D. Cicchetti & D.J. Cohen (pp. 96–161). New York: Wiley.

Rohrbeck, C.A., Ginsburg-Block, M.D., Fantuzzo, J.W., & Miller, T.R. (2003). Peer-assisted learning interventions with elementary school students: A meta-analytic review. *Journal of Educational Psychology*, 95(2): 240–257.

Rousseau, J.-J. (1921). *Emile, or Education*. Trans. B. Foxley. London & Toronto: J.M. Dent and Sons; New York: E.P. Dutton.

Conclusion

The almost complete absence, for over a century of psychology, of psychoanalytical-developmental attention to the latency age both on the level of therapy and on the educational level has led to therapeutic and educational approaches that are not based on knowledge and understanding of the developmental processes that occur during this age. This creates a lack of direction, where we wander in the darkness without a beam of light to illuminate the road that has always existed.

This book has presented a developmental-psychoanalytical paradigm showing that during latency an impressive development occurs with the emergence of a new part of the self: the social self, which includes the function of subordination. This development includes the characteristics of age-related development: gender separation, asexuality, group friendships, stereotypes, social hierarchy, social norms, social rejection, and social empathy and morality.

According to the paradigm presented in this book, the latency stage leads to the next stage, adolescence. From this stage onwards, people are subject to a reality where the self includes two essences, the childhood self and the social self, with a membrane translating between the two. With the establishment of a social moral system during latency, from adolescence onwards people are able to choose freely between two moral systems. One is the generic morality of the superego and the family, which is finite, fixed, and inflexible. The other is the social morality, which is infinite, flexible, and relative, and includes social norms that change.

In all the early development stages up to the end of the Oedipal stage, the children's psyches existed in the willfulness function of the self core, which involves the psyche's grandiosity, omnipotence, and focus on object control. During latency, the psyche moves into the social self cytoplasm, where the self core is blocked and becomes unconscious and the psyche's function is subordination.

When children have deficits from earlier stages, they continue to exist in the childhood self during latency, in the self core with the function of psychic willfulness, and usually suffer from social rejection. The socially rejected children often insist on doing things their way, emphasizing their will exclusively, and are unable to accept social situations where another child is the center of the social world, makes decisions and is in control, and the other children have to subordinate themselves to those higher in the class hierarchy and to accept social norms decided by the independent society of children. These children often encounter situations where they distort reality and try to change the rules to be "winners", demonstrating their power as part of their inability to handle their inferiority in the face of other children's strong abilities and wills. They obey generic rules. They show dependence upon adults' authority and require their help in coping with social situations. They obey parents and teachers and usually act in contrast to the social norms in their class (such as informing to the teacher). They usually see themselves as "good" and the society of children as "bad", and the teachers and parents support this view. They don't behave in accordance with the age's characteristics: boys and girls play together, and their behavior sometimes doesn't match their class's gender stereotypes. They often seek out interpersonal friendships with a "best friend" and feel betrayed if their friend prefers group-hierarchical friendship.

Developmental difficulties during latency may lead to problems later in life, with a focus on personal needs and desires rather than on the social context. At the end of latency, from adolescence onwards, people move between the two psychic functions of willfulness and subordination. The former is infantile, interpersonal, and uncompromising, as the personal will is grandiose and omnipotent, and the expectation is that the environment is controlled and helps the individual achieve his or her personal goals and desires. This is a position where morality is absolute, unchanging, iron-clad, and deterministic. The latter function is social, and its nature changes. In this function, the psyche moves flexibly and adapts itself to the environment. It acts in a socially adaptive manner. Its morality is relative, noncompulsory, compromising, and changes according to social circumstances. As adults, we need to have sharp social sensors to perceive social behavior patterns in order to achieve our personal goals or wishes.

When the subordination function doesn't develop due to deficits in the early stages, self-focused people develop values that usually have the quality of a rigid, uncompromising superego. They can be very empathic, with a spontaneous, emotional ability to identify, but they lack the ability to be flexible and give up their personal needs and desires when other factors should be considered and it's necessary to act flexibly in a way that might differ from their personal instinct, drive, or desire. Such people's goals and decisions are deterministic. They can't help providing for their personal needs and making choices deriving from the need to compensate for early childhood deficits. Their sensitivity to others, emotional empathy, and emotional morality will not enable them to choose. They will identify totally with the suffering of others and won't be able to consider other factors, such as the way expressing empathy may hurt dignity.

The development of the subordination function in the social self cytoplasm is the most significant of all the age's occurrences. This is a development that "complicates" human existence and makes it fascinating and complex. It adds a layer of infinity, thus making the self into a dual system: finite and infinite; absolute and relative; "particle" and "wave" in quantum physics. This complementary contrast creates such a complex and multifaceted human psychic existence that we must express astonished gratitude for our incredible creation. The purpose of therapy and educational approaches is to enable this development, and, no less important, not to harm or delay this development. Adults can harm the developmental process when they encourage latency age children to insist on their own will and not to subordinate themselves; to fight the class rulers; to hold onto their values; to have one "best friend" or an opposite sex friend; to refuse to accept the social hierarchy; to continue obeying the parents' and teachers authority, rules, and values; to be "good" children and avoid the company of "bad" children; or to protest or avoid obeying latency age social norms.

The book presents a psychological therapy method based on the developmental paradigm, aimed at helping socially rejected children to develop flexibility within the function of willfulness and to choose and control their movement between two possibilities: being socially accepted while making a "difficult" decision to surrender personal desires, or not to surrender personal wishes, which leads to the "difficult" situation of social rejection.

The educational approach according to the developmental paradigm places the class's development as an autonomous group at the center of the school experience. An independently operating class with its own unique hierarchy, norms, language, and behavior is what enables the children to develop in all areas during latency. The social space of an autonomous class, with the homeroom teachers supporting and helping its development, is an appropriate growing structure for psychic development during latency, in the new psychic space of the social self cytoplasm with the subordination function.

Index

www.ingramcontent.com/pod-product-compliance
Ingram Content Group UK Ltd.
Pitfield, Milton Keynes, MK11 3LW, UK
UKHW020421010325
455677UK00029B/961